BORDERLINE
and BEYOND

Expanded 2007 Edition
Applies to BPD/ASD

LAURA PAXTON

White Tiger
Dream Press

TABLE OF CONTENTS

BORDERLINE
and BEYOND

Expanded 2007 Edition
Applies to BPD/ASD

Evolution of the Borderline and Beyond Program

When I wrote the original edition of *Borderline and Beyond* in 1996, my primary focus was helping BPD sufferers begin to take personal responsibility for recovery. For me, this was the only way out of "the borderline hell." I still consider making the transition from "victim identity" to "responsible, empowered identity" to be critical to the recovery process. On this day in 2006, I also want to add something else a bit new. We define who we are through our personal choices. Having a sense of identity is dependent upon our ability to sort out for ourselves what we want, what we believe, and what we choose to do as a result.

Some people are very sensitive to the opinions of others, and they change their opinions of themselves dependent upon the opinions and perceptions of the people they happen to be around. They are not actively making behavioral choices that allow them to define themselves. Often, these people are labeled as having "borderline personality disorder." Most of the nine criteria used to diagnose borderline personality disorder are based upon behavioral choices. Any five of the nine result in diagnosis. Choices can be changed, if a person suffering from BPD really wants to change badly enough. In 1996, I reached that point of dedication to change, and since then, I have not met the criteria for BPD.

I have not had empirical studies done to show whether or not my program (which was first released in 1999) works for others, but the ongoing positive response I have received reflects its helpfulness to many people. In the future, it may be possible for me to conduct research in order to document results empirically.

Marsha Linehan's program, Dialectical Behavior Therapy (DBT,) has had success in proving results in recovery.[1] However, cognitive behavioral approaches[2] and psychodynamic approaches (such as TFP: Transference Focused Psychotherapy)[3] have recently been proven to be effective for others in recovery, although (to this date) no comparative analysis of TFP to DBT has been completed. My program complements any of the above programs and is often used in conjunction with them. Many people also use this book as a "stand alone" program, and have reported positive results.

My 2004 revised edition of *Borderline and Beyond* had a strong emphasis on the role of spirituality in recovery. I still believe this is a powerful part of the healing process. I still use meditation, biofeedback and mindfulness techniques in my daily life. I take time out each day to focus on gratitude, prayer and focusing on doing nurturing and loving things for myself. My biggest problem was that I was such a strong believer in positive thinking that I believed it was the answer to everything.

In June of 2005, I had a dream that a child came to me and showed me two dollhouses. One of them was in pieces on the floor. The other, she handed to me intact, right before it shattered in my hands. I asked her, "Is there going to be another death?" She responded, "Yes." So, I asked, "Am I going to die?" Her only response was, "It has something to do with sense."

She disappeared, just as there was a knock at the door. I answered it, and it was my maternal grandmother. I asked her if she was there to take me with her to heaven. She responded, "No. It isn't time for that yet. Rest in eternal life." The door closed. I looked around the room and saw that green plants were growing everywhere as the brightest light that I have ever seen before was streaming through the windows.

As I discussed this dream with my father later, he wondered whether the dream had to do with some sort of "ego death." In 1996, I underwent a very real sort of "death." I had intentionally overdosed on medication and spent time in ICU before being transported to a state mental hospital. I felt clearly at that time that life as I had known it had to die. I had to give up most of my old way of thinking and behaving, realizing that it was my only chance to get better. It was during this period of time that I developed the original *Borderline and Beyond Program.*

Ten years later, through the process of living 2005-2006, a similar, (yet less dramatic) death occurred. I was not hospitalized again. I did not self-injure. I did not threaten suicide, although ideation did occur at times. I did not feel abandoned. I did not feel "empty" inside. Then again, I have never in my life really felt "empty," only miserable at times. But, this time, I was definitely in a state of life crisis. Everything I believed about myself so strongly for so many years completely collapsed.

It took about a year for me to develop my own new paradigm, to replace what I had lost. During that more challenging year, I lost enthusiasm for the entire subject of borderline personality disorder. I stopped my monthly workshops and retreat programs. I did not update my web-site. Regularly, I would receive e-mails, asking such questions as, "What happened to you?"

"What happened to me," is this: I completely stopped identifying with the construct of BPD. I was tired of it, after spending a decade focused on research and education on the subject. I even stopped identifying with being a "poster child of recovery," or a "recovered person with BPD."

I learned that in order to cope with my life, and in order to stop displaying the behaviors that met the BPD criteria, I needed consciously and diligently to practice new skills and behaviors. I did this until the routines became habits. Eventually, the habits felt automatic to me, and I no longer needed to focus on them. I do not believe that I am "like an alcoholic on the wagon" with BPD recovery. I don't think it has the ability to creep up and take over my life again. I feel completed with that entire phase of my life. I am the type of person who will always do my best with what I have. I did my best with what I had until I learned coping skills to control the BPD. The problem was, nine years later, I did not understand why I would still "stress out" when faced with changes and transitions to new situations.

I had learned to maintain a very serene equilibrium and a deep sense of inner peace. But, each time the setting of my life was radically changed, I would need time to "re-stabilize" inside. Despite my best effort, sometimes I was still confronted with the sense of "overwhelm" to stimuli and stress, which resulted in anxiety and depression. I did not understand until recently that this is because of the way I process sensory experiences (as my previous dream about "sense" had suggested!) I was not "doing something wrong" in psychological process work or spiritual process.

I developed shingles twice in my mid-thirties, and I am not immune-suppressed. I was having occasional panic attacks so severe that I called 911 on more than one occasion. I was getting sick more than the average person would, with bronchitis, migraines, and neuralgia (which is a lingering byproduct of my past bouts with shingles.) At times, my migraines would occur 3-5 times a week.

In 2005, I underwent a deep personal crisis. The stress in my life exceeded my ability to cope with it. Still, I did not behave in a "borderline manner." I realized I needed to explore other possibilities of why I could not cope with this stress. Finally, I sought out a series of neuropsychological assessments. The result was a gradual unveiling of some very "enlightening" discoveries about myself.

After a full year of various assessments and treatment experiences, I was finally diagnosed to have a "high functioning autism spectrum disorder."

At 37 years of age, I learned that I have autism. After this, the entire story of my life began to make perfect sense. I gained a new appreciation and respect for my own challenges, as I also began to learn new approaches for coping with them. Never before had I realized how profoundly the difference is between the way I perceive and process the world, and the way other people do.

Each autistic person is very different. I have often heard that, "If you've seen one autistic, you've seen one autistic." Some autistic people think completely in pictures. Some are mathematical geniuses. Others are musical prodigies. Some talk and some do not. Autism spans a full range from mentally retarded to genius level I.Q. It is usually marked by an imbalance in skills or intelligence. Whatever that particular imbalance happens to be makes communication and forming relationships with others more difficult. This is because other people cannot easily relate to a person who does not have a more even profile of abilities.

Most people with autism spectrum disorders also have sensory "issues," such as hyper or hypo-sensitivity. Studies cite percentages of autistics who also have sensory integration disorder at 80-87%.[4] However, many people without autism also have sensory issues. For example, 39.5% of those diagnosed with attention deficit disorder are "tactile defensive," meaning that they have sensory issues surrounding the sense of touch.[5] Although at least 13% of those with autism have no severe sensory complaints at all, for me and for many other autistic adults, the sensory differences we experience comprise some of our greatest challenges in relating to others.

In my specific case of autism, my mind does not at all "make maps" of what I see. I sometimes read nonverbal communication about like a blind person would, but my social skills are currently so good that even non-verbal learning disability was almost never considered for me. My intelligence and the broad range of strategies I have used are all adaptations. I feel I have a good intuition with people. Still, I ask questions, so that I'm not making assumptions about what they are thinking and feeling.

Interpretation of non-verbal behavior has been a hard-earned skill, and one that I am still working to improve. I spent my childhood eating lunch and playing alone, kindergarten through high school. My clinical presentation as a child might have resembled Asperger's Disorder (one form of high functioning autism,) if that relatively new diagnosis had been given to children at that time. In my difficult process of coping through most of my twenties, I struggled with what was labeled "borderline personality disorder." My social skills development was not distorted as much as it was merely delayed. I only started to blossom in social skills development in my early thirties, after I got the BPD symptoms under control.

After receiving my original diagnosis of NLD (nonverbal learning disability,) I spent sixteen sessions in therapy with a psychologist who specialized in helping patients sort out neuropsychological issues and the accompanying anxiety they cause. His conclusion was that I probably had Asperger's Disorder, and he referred me to get another assessment done. This assessment (which was cursory and not very thorough!) still did not find Asperger's, but it did find the possibility of Sensory Integration Disorder (SID,) and I was referred to occupational therapy. SID was diagnosed there and I began an intensive rehabilitation program.

After five months of seeing a psychiatrist who also specialized in neuropsychiatry, he concluded that it is impossible that I have Bipolar Disorder, type I or II. Instead, he decided that I suffer from ADD, Type II, the "inattentive" rather than the "hyperactive" type. My pattern in life was to launch into an enthusiastic project, dedicating all of my energy to it, but then enter into a distractible phase, unable to manage the details. Finally, I crashed with anxiety and depression. I moved from an over-focused phase to highly distracted phase, characteristic of ADD. During this phase, I could not manage the details of my business.

After I came to be reliably diagnosed with non-verbal learning disability, attention deficit disorder-inattentive type, and sensory integration disorder, I still felt something was very amiss. I had come to identify with Asperger's Disorder and had even joined a support group for it. None of my new friends whom I met at these meetings could believe that I did not have Asperger's Syndrome also. So, I arranged for a private evaluation with a double board certified M.D. who specialized in autism spectrum disorders. After a year of work in therapy and multiple assessments, I finally received the diagnosis. Verbally, he told me, "Asperger's Syndrome, Moderate." My report simply states, "High Functioning Autism."

At this point, I immediately found intense relief for what had been an unknown lifelong stress. Receiving appropriate diagnosis and treatment (for the significant stress my unidentified condition caused) has been restoring me to overall improved cognitive functioning, resulting in a sense of wholeness. I still believe that our choice of thought process can dramatically affect our psychological and physical health. However, I have also had an increasing interest in biochemistry, neurology and neuropsychology over the past year.

If a part of the brain is not functioning properly, meditating for hours on end is going to be just as effective as spending a day meditating on moving a mountain. In fact, meditation is sometimes counter-productive or even contra-indicated with patients who present with the constellation of borderline traits. One reason for this is that escapism or dissociation is often encouraged.

Great advances in medicine have been made over the past decade, so there is no reason not to take advantage of them. They can help to correct brain functioning which has been dysfunctional for years. The effect for me of finally receiving a proper diagnosis and treatment has been like slowly feeling my brain (and senses!) "wake up" so that I can participate in the world more fully.

When I wrote the first edition of Borderline and Beyond, I was taking Zoloft and Depakote. When I wrote the updated edition in 2001 and in 2004, I was taking no medications at all, but only dedicating myself to prayer, meditation and spiritual practice. Some of the effects of this were very dramatic and have lasted to this day. Even without taking medications for six years, I did not "act like a borderline."

I want to emphasize strongly that taking medications from 1996-1999 was the only way I could accomplish enough emotional stability to move forward in my life, without continuing the old "borderline" pattern. Now, I am taking medications again, but for completely different reasons. Many people have strong feelings about the subject of psychiatric medications. In address to these people, I will briefly list a few of the things I tried before making my decision to surrender to medication treatment: I tried meditation, biofeedback, yoga, raw food, all organic food, gluten free diet and a plethora of herbal supplements. I still do most of these things, along with taking medication. I agree that if a natural alternative is possible, try it first, unless your condition is severe or life threatening. I add the caveat that one should not hesitate to take psychiatric medications if they are needed or helpful, any more than one should hesitate to take medication for diabetes or a heart condition.

However, I view my condition as 80% neurological, and 20% psychological. As my evaluating psychiatrist explained, the Asperger's Syndrome was primary and BPD secondary. Young people today who are being identified as having Asperger's are at a definite advantage. Hopefully, fewer of them will go on to develop personality disorders, because they will receive enough assistance through special education to cope more with issues related to AS.

Other good news is that although Asperger's is not "curable," the problematic symptoms I've experienced are now being treated, and I am deeply relieved to be getting better. In addition to medications, my treatment regimen includes nutritional supplements, a (mostly) gluten free diet, occupational therapy and weekly sessions with my very excellent psychiatrist. He has helped me learn to accept and cope with my condition better.

The combination of Asperger's Syndrome (AS,) NLD, SID and ADD, with the accompanying major anxiety they caused together should have disabled me throughout my life far more than they have. However, I became a "master compensator." In my thirties, I began to learn more social skills.

For the first time in my life, I could not only appear "normal," but super-normal. My period of great achievement in my work was also accompanied with a secret stress, which I hid, rather than seeking treatment. It has taken me 37 years to get accurate assessment and treatment for the underlying causes of what may have led to my meeting the criteria for borderline personality disorder, between the years of

15 and 26. No one would listen to me or take me seriously when I repeatedly complained about my disorientation and social confusion. I actually gave up on psychiatric treatment when I was 26, and decided that if I was going to get better, I had to do it all by myself. However, a decade later, I did reach a point where I learned that it was safe to reach out to the medical community for help again.

One of the reasons why I delayed getting treatment was that at least a dozen times in my twenties, I had expressed concerns to my psychiatrists about my neurological functioning. Every single time, my requests were dismissed as "histrionic," "borderline," or "like a hypochondriac." Nobody took me seriously enough even to offer a neurological exam or thorough neuropsychological testing. In fact, ten years after my recovery from BPD, the first clinic I finally had the courage to go back to repeated this trauma. The psychologist actually said to me, "From your past history, I can tell you that most of your problems are bound to be personality related. I don't think you need neuropsychological testing. But, if you insist, we can provide that."

Obviously, I felt insulted, after all the hard work I had done over the past decade, not only to maintain my recovery, but also to work to be a positive role model for others. Of course, I did not trust this clinic, due to its apparent bias. When I discovered a neuro-psychologist who would take my symptoms seriously, I was 36 years old. I was 37 before I learned that I also had high functioning autism. Like most autistics, I have some "obsessive-compulsive seeming" traits. Some of my rituals and routines are necessary for me to keep my bearings in a world that feels spatially disorienting to me. Some of my behaviors are "overkill," but these have subsided quite a bit with therapy.

Although the psychologist who tested me in November, 2005 DID take my symptoms seriously, he believed my social skills were too high for an autism spectrum diagnosis. Despite this, my difficulties with reading nonverbal communication and not being able to communicate my emotions when I was upset continued. So, several months later, I was informed in another assessment that my personality problems were primary and the neurological problems were secondary. I received my report three months after the evaluation. The report was full of inaccuracies and misquotes. The cursory attention given to my case was evident.

I sought a second opinion through the double board certified psychiatrist who specialized in autism spectrum disorders. At first, he stated that co-morbidity between AS and BPD had not been established. He performed a literature review and saw the array of cases that did have both diagnoses. After intensive interviewing and review of a plethora or records (including baby books and visual media of my childhood,) this doctor diagnosed me with an autism spectrum disorder without question. Again, this doctor stated that I also did not currently meet the criteria for borderline personality disorder.

Since this time, I discovered that three women in my Asperger's support group were previously labeled as being "borderline," when they were in their mid-20's. The difference was that they never mentioned it during their assessment for Asperger's. Of course, due to the familiarity of so many professionals with my work, my past had to be brought up. Ten years ago, my problems could be described more as 50% psychological and 50% neurological. I had not worked through the trauma-related issues that I did have to the degree that I have today. Since I was completely unaware that I had neurological impairments, I wasted energy extensively through the years. I struggled with futility to treat undetected neurological problems with a purely psychological approach, followed by a spiritual approach.

Spiritual approaches have been one critical factor in successful recovery for most people who have fully recovered from "BPD." However, this disorder is one of the most complex of all the psychiatric diagnoses. Medication treatment and appropriate therapy are essential when one reaches a point severe enough to be labeled "BPD." Although, for a year now, I have undergone a complete re-evaluation of myself and my relationship to "BPD," I still care about advocacy for people who receive the borderline personality diagnostic label. Because of my personal experience, I am including information in this edition about how neurological issues may be the primary source of how and why borderline personality disorder develops in many patients.

I believe these issues are too often overlooked. It is possible that if I had received correct diagnosis and treatment twenty years ago, I would probably never have arrived at such an out-of-control state that I met the criteria for BPD, during the years that I did. I might not have then spent a decade of my life suffering from BPD, and then another decade of my life using the wrong tools to cope with the underlying problems.

Now, ten years after my original writing of *Borderline and Beyond* in 1996, and exactly one year after my dream about the house collapsing, I am building a "new house." I only hope and pray that if a third house needs to be built ten years from now, that I will sustain the stamina to do it. Through this updated edition, up to 40% of the content has been changed. However, I have preserved the "most loved" sections of the original version. I have carefully kept all the material that I received the most positive feedback about regarding its helpfulness.

Note, 1/3/07: I have recently been declared to NOT have ADD, but to have Mood Disorder, NOS. My medications were changed and I am much happier. As one can see, differentiating the difference often takes much clinical skill and often consultation with multiple doctors.

This remainder of this new edition is divided into only two parts:
(1) Changing Viewpoints About The BPD Diagnosis and (2) The Borderline and Beyond Program.

We'll begin with Part I:

Changing
    Viewpoints
        about
            The BPD
                Diagnosis

Quotes: Current Professional Views of BPD

- "Borderline personality disorder is at best a confusing concept, and at worst, a counter-transference diagnosis,[6][7] which robs the patient of the opportunity of much needed treatment."

-Hagop Akisal, M.D.[8]

- "Clearly, then, the diagnosis of BPD is more variable over time than the *DSM-IV* generic criterion of longitudinal stability would imply. Other studies have shown similar results." (Lenzenweger, 1999[9]; Zanarini et al., 2003[10]).-

-John M. Oldham, M.D., (who chaired the workgroup for the APA that developed the practice guideline for the treatment of patients with BPD.)[11]

- "Segregating people with personality disorders onto Axis II harms them clinically and economically while thwarting the development of new research and dissemination of knowledge. It gives managed care companies an excuse for withholding payments to persons with personality disorders. It also encourages misdiagnosis as clinicians often prefer their patients receive insurance coverage rather than an accurate diagnosis."

- Roger Peele, MD, LDFAPA, Chief Psychiatrist, Montgomery County, Maryland and Area III Consultant for BPD Practice Guidelines[12]

- "The name BPD is confusing, imparts no relevant or descriptive information, and reinforces existing stigma."

-Valerie Porr, M.A.,[13] President of TARA- APD[14]

- "Apparently the greatest sin a patient can commit is the sin of poor response to treatment."

-Joel Dvoskin, PhD Assistant Clinical Professor   of Psychiatry, University of Arizona College of Medicine, Tucson, AZ.[15]

- "Borderline personality disorder is one of the most commonly overused diagnoses in *DSM-IV*"

-David Bienenfeld, MD, Vice-Chair, Program Director, Professor, Department of Psychiatry, Wright State University School of Medicine[16]

- "We submit that the construct of borderline personality disorder is better covered by more conventional diagnostic entities."

-Perugi G, Toni C, Travierso MC, Akiskal[17]

The Stigma of Borderline Personality Disorder (BPD)

For years, those diagnosed with borderline personality disorder have felt as if they were just given the "kiss of death." They have been told that they are suffering from a disorder which is difficult, if not impossible, to treat. BPD is an illness that drives other people away just when they need those people most.

Persons suffering from BPD have also been told that they may never experience all of the emotions mature adults are able to experience, and that they may never experience the degrees of intimacy that other adults are capable of. It has even been postulated that as the illness appears to "mellow" or stabilize somewhat in middle age, "Some observers believe these people have achieved self-command and self-control by forgoing the intimacy that was both an imperative need and an intolerable burden for them in youth."[18] What a sacrifice for these individuals to feel they have to make!

As Associate Clinical Professor of Psychiatry at the Harvard Medical School, Judith Lewis Herman, M.D., so astutely comments, the term borderline personality disorder is "frequently used within the mental health professions as little more than a sophisticated insult."[19]

Individuals suffering from borderline personality disorder have often been treated as psychiatric lepers, with treating professionals approaching them armored with rigid boundaries, negative expectations, and a poor prognosis. This does not need to be the case. Another alternative exists: to see the individual suffering from this disorder as courageous and full of creative potential.

Since the Borderline and Beyond Program was first published in 1999, I have consistently received multiple e-mails each month from people who were misinformed by their psychiatrist or therapist that BPD is not treatable or curable. Many of these were taken off their psychiatric medications by psychiatrists who simply "gave up" or refused to treat them. This continues to occur, seven years later, because not all professionals are "up-to-date" about the improved prognosis for recovery from BPD.

One of the most touching phone calls I received was from a woman who had recently been told that she was diagnosed BPD and that there was no effective treatment. She planned to kill herself in response, until she visited my web-site, where she was able to see that I and many other people have recovered from BPD. Often, spouses write stating that their marriage and family therapist advised them to end their marriage or relationship because their partner is borderline. Again, this does not take into account that many people with BPD do recover.

There is even a set of practice guidelines published by the American Psychiatric Association that are designed to be used with patients who have BPD,[20] but many psychiatrists I have spoken with are not familiar with them. Therefore, it is essential that you seek licensed mental health care providers who have a positive and realistic approach to treating this disorder.

My book, *Borderline and Beyond*, was one of the first books to challenge the assumption that BPD could not be overcome. In 2002, I also wrote the original forward for Rachel Reiland's book, *I'm Not Supposed to Be Here*,[21] later published by Hazelden as *Get Me Out of Here*.[22] My forward was replaced by that of Jerold Kreisman, M.D. I was proud of Rachel's book, and how she contributed to the belief that recovery is possible from BPD. Also in 2002, the book, *New Hope for Borderline Personality*, entered the market.[23] Attitudes in the psychiatric community began to change a great deal.

Despite these hopeful changes, the Diagnostic and Statistical Manual (DSM) committee has no definite plan to place BPD on Axis I, where so many patients and professionals believe it should really be. Axis II conditions are chronic, pervasive conditions that are not considered likely to change. People with the BPD label often do change. Therefore, placing this vaguely understood and ill-defined disorder on Axis II does little but to stigmatize those suffering from it and often (as in my case) interfere with more appropriate diagnosis and treatment.

Regardless of how you are labeled or not labeled, the most important concept for you to remember is this: Your life choices determine who you are. My hope is that the individual who has been diagnosed with borderline personality disorder may read this book and find resources and strengths that exceed what was previously believed to be possible. The inevitable result of making more responsible choices is the emergence of positive feelings of pride, confidence and contentment within one's self image.

Changing Views of
Borderline Personality Disorder

What is the core underlying psychological dynamic that contributes to borderline behavior? In other words, "Exactly what makes a 'borderline' a 'borderline?'" I was diagnosed under the DSM-III criteria. At this time, there were only 8 criteria, not 9, as there are today. This criteria did not include the criterion believed to be highly significant when the DSM-IV was published. According to Andrew Skodol, M.D., Criterion #9 was added because 75% of those diagnosed with BPD also had "transient, stress-related paranoid ideation or severe dissociative symptoms." This particular symptom was reported to have "excellent specificity" i.e. rarely occurring in other diagnostic groups. He cited nine research studies to back up this assertion, all of which occurred prior to 1991.[24]

In 1991, Judith Herman, M.D. explicated how criterion #9 actually appears in four other disorders, besides BPD. In 1992, she published a new criteria and name for BPD. In her book, *Trauma and Recovery*, she delineated   a far more specific, recommended DSM criteria for the diagnosis she termed "Complex Post-Traumatic Stress Disorder."

Herman effectively delineated how BPD presents itself in the context of trauma. However, one of the most common myths and assumptions about BPD is that it is usually, if not always, based on trauma. Often, it is not at all. In fact, the most recent study (Zweig-Frank, 2006) found that there is no link whatsoever between PTSD and BPD.[25] The 2003 Golier study had reflected the same conclusion. Only 53% of the large BPD sample reported abuse. (Other studies have shown the incidence of childhood sexual abuse to be as low as 40%.[26])

In the Golier study, their findings showed sufficient evidence to reflect that borderline personality disorder is NOT a trauma spectrum disorder.[27] Similar results were shown in a 2000 empirical investigation. "Identity disturbance appears to be characteristic of BPD patients, whether or not they have an abuse history," concluded Wilkinson-Ryan, PhD and Drew Weston PhD.[28]

The most popular current theory is that the most central diagnostic criterion is #7, "Affective instability due to a marked reactivity of mood (e.g., intense episodic dysphoria, irritability, or anxiety usually lasting a few hours and only rarely more than a few days)." This is one reason why Marsha Linehan, PhD, has proposed "Emotion Regulation Disorder" as a more appropriate diagnostic label for BPD.

Hagop S. Akisal M.D. believes that BPD should be included in the bipolar spectrum.[29] After all, even from Linehan's description, core characteristics of BPD are related to mood. Akisal believes that as many as 80% of people diagnosed with BPD have bipolar spectrum qualities, although many show only "soft bipolarity," which is usually associated with Type II Bipolar Disorder.

Within type II, more severe depressive episodes are interspersed with periods of "hypomania," or more agitated or elated phases that do not meet the criteria for full manic episode. Because of the degree of overlap between Bipolar, type II and BPD, Akisal believes that BPD would be better classified as an Axis II mood disorder.[30]

To refute this, in a review paper published by the *Canadian Journal of Psychiatry*, August 2004, a committee decided that BPD should maintain its integrity as a diagnostic entity, for the following reason:

> The BPD group scored significantly higher on harm avoidance, impulsivity, and disorderliness and lower on self-directedness, cooperativeness, and persistence. The ability to distinguish BPD patients and BD patients according to deviations in temperament and character supports the notion that BPD is not simply a variant of BD[31].

However, Akisal states[32] that,

> "In a New Zealand study[33], BPD was characterized by high novelty seeking and harm avoidance, and low self-directedness and low cooperativeness – the same profile has been found for the cyclothymic temperament[34].

"Self-directedness" clearly stands out in both studies as a central piece of the "borderline personality" profile. I agree that learning how to achieve a sense of "self-directedness" is probably one of the most essential skills to develop in recovery.

However, as Akisal points out above, "low self-directedness" is also associated with "cyclothymic temperment." Based upon this, I am not convinced that BPD has much integrity at all as a separate diagnostic entity. I am also not convinced that it is always a variant of a mood disorder, either. Other studies have showed co-morbidity of BPD with Bipolar Disorder as low as only 19.4%[35]. I believe that in many cases, BPD may be a variant of Bipolar II. For others, BPD presents itself as the primary result of psychological trauma or from right hemisphere processing problems.

Emotional Dysregulation Disorder alone does not seem to be an adequate label to give to patients who present the BPD profile. Emotional dysregulation is also present in a variety of other conditions, including NLD, SID, ADD and the autistic spectrum disorders. More specifically, NLD, ADD and SID are all believed to result from right hemisphere dysfunction. The similarities to the neurology of BPD are actually uncanny.In fact, a May 2006 study, "Missing Links in Borderline Personality Disorder: Loss of Neural Synchrony Relates to Lack of Emotional Regulation and Impulse Control," researchers Leanne M. Williams, M.D, Anna Sidis, M.D.; Evian Gordon, M.D. and Russell A. Meares, M.D. postulated this:

In patients with BPD with greater variation in affective dysregulation, we would hypothesize a further association between these symptoms and right hemisphere breakdowns in gamma integration.[36]By "gamma integration," the researchers were referring to their use of "gamma" as a resolution measure of brain activity. They also postulated that, "Symptoms of borderline personality disorder (BPD) may reflect distinct breakdowns in the integration of posterior and frontal brain networks."[37]With diagnostic criterion #3, "unstable sense of identity," researchers identified the elements of identity disturbances as role absorption (defining self in terms of a role or cause,) a subjective sense of "lack of coherence," inconsistency in thought, feeling and behavior, and lack of commitment (e.g. to jobs or values.)[38]

These four criterion may also be the result of neurological conditions, such as ADD, OCD, NLD or Asperger's Syndrome. People who live with these styles of neurological functioning often have great difficulty sustaining employment or believing that they can accomplish career goals. Values may change due to distractibility, experimentation or other causes. An individual with a right hemisphere related syndrome is generally not able to experience a "subjective sense of inner coherence."

A recent psychiatric conference probed the "Awareness of Self Awareness." Michael Jonathan Grinfeld reported on the conference and its conclusions in a recent article:

> The absence of an accepted definition of self-awareness that could encompass all of its elements led to its representation in the form of the simple question posed at the beginning of the conference, said Jyotsna Nair, M.D., a speaker at the conference and assistant professor of psychiatry at the University of Missouri, Columbia, Health Sciences Center. "Self-awareness depends on a person developing more than just a concept of self, but also requires memory, language, awareness of body and the ability to form some sort of presentation of yourself," she told the attendees. "The concept of self is an evolving process that changes. It changes every day, every moment, even into old age."
>
> The inability of patients with schizophrenia, autism, personality disorders, attention-deficit/hyperactivity disorder, hysteria and substance abuse disorders to fathom their impact on the people who surround them or to recognize

that their thoughts fail to conform to the realities of their lives has a negative impact on the course of treatment and decreases the likelihood that any intervention will achieve improved functioning. While psychiatrists have known for a long time that denial or lack of insight can undermine treatment, this conference sought to focus on deficits in self-awareness as pathology.[39]

Rather than single out borderline personality disorder as the primary or only illness in which deficits of self-concept or seen, this particular conference focused on more expansive applications of the concept.

While lack of a sense of identity is not a diagnostic construct specific only to "borderline personality disorder," predominant in the psychopathology of borderline personality disorder is the issue of "invited victimization." I find it incomprehensible that this is not listed at all in the diagnostic criteria for BPD. Jerold Kreisman, M.D. writes in his best-selling book about BPD, *I Hate You-Don't Leave Me: Understanding Borderline Personality Disorder* that "a pattern of invited victimization is often a hallmark of BPD."[40] Women who are diagnosed with BPD are prone to relationships with abusive men. They often report a long history of repetition trauma in their adult lives with multiple life situations.

I believe that many people suffering from BPD tend to identify strongly with feeling like victims. A central diagnostic feature of borderline patients is considered to be a lack of firm, central sense of identity. Often overlooked is the strong identification with the "victim position" that will prevail throughout multiple apparent shifts of identification with various life roles and descriptions.

Borderline identity is victim identity. People diagnosed with BPD have a firm, central sense of themselves as life's victims. People with BPD do have an identity, through this consistent "victim-self" structure that allows them to organize life experience. Although borderline identity is "victim identity," this role can actually be shifted through proper treatment.

The "victim identity" often crystallizes into a chronic, rigid pattern over time, as patients seek help and learn to feel more helpless and less enabled as a result. This may occur for many reasons, other than poor diagnosis and treatment. Some people who are diagnosed as borderline personality disorder have experienced repeated traumatic experiences. They were often victimized as children, so "victim identity" is the only identity they have. They feel no other choice but to be passive, needy and frozen, as they re-live the only experiences familiar to them.

Many people with mood disorders do not receive appropriate diagnosis and treatment. A 1998 Canadian study showed that it may take an average of as long as four years to receive an appropriate disagnosis of schizophrenia, and 12.5 years to receive an accurate mood disorder diagnosis.[41]

A 2004 USA study conducted by DBSA (Depression and Bipolar Support Alliance) estimated the average number of years of struggle before receiving the correct diagnosis of bipolar disorder as "ten." The most disturbing part was that 75% had been misdiagnosed 1-3 times before receiving appropriate treatment.[42]

As complex and difficult as bipolar disorder is to diagnose, mis-application of the construct of "borderline personality disorder" is like the bipolar misdiagnosis exponentialized. The criteria are more broad and open to interpretation, and they require detailed history-taking that patients aren't always able to cooperate with. So, after multiple medication trials have failed, these patients may feel a profound sense of just wanting to "give up."

Many other individuals, such as myself, have underlying neurological conditions that interfere with normal right hemisphere processing. At times, the result may easily create a picture that fits the criteria for BPD. Emotional and sensory modulation problems are common. Impulsiveness is common. Difficulty navigating through social situations is common. Over a period of time, when these issues are not addressed or are mislabeled and not treated properly, symptoms tend to worsen.

There was a point when I "gave up" and began to attach to a "victim identity." It was during that time that I was diagnosed with BPD. When I was assessed in November, 2005, my report stated that I was "far less impulsive than other individuals with NLD." However, I was once extremely impulsive. Taking Depakote for a while curbed some of these tendencies for me. At the same time, I began practicing mindfulness and I became more aware of my choices and ability to choose my actions. The direct opposite of "victim mentality" is a "self-directed" mentality. I have worked hard through the years to generate a sense of my own inner power and direction. The results have paid off extremely well.

I am rarely impulsive now, but I have had to work very hard for my recovery, especially during the early phases of recovery and later during times of life stress. That is why I've stressed repeatedly how much energy it takes to sustain a commitment to recovery and to do what it takes to maintain it each day. Replacing the "victim mentality" with a sense of inner power and direction is the pivotal point of change. I also believe that if borderline personality disorder has any true validity as a diagnostic entity, the "strong sense that our decisions create our identity" is the most central facet to both diagnosis and treatment.

I also have been diagnosed with major depression, recurrent. So, I do fit somewhere on the mood disorder continuum, although I am not bipolar. I did experience a few traumatic childhood incidents. I have had extensive therapy for them. But, the core issue was that my ADD probably needed medication treatment.

Also, my autism, with its SID and NLD components, has required the help of an occupational therapist. So, for me, I needed a different central "starting place" to make my work in recovery easier. Despite these additions, today, my recovery program is actually less work. My new program frees me to do more productive things with my life than to stew in sensory or emotional overload.

Many different paths lead eventually to the borderline personality diagnosis. In each individual case, the root cause of the dysfunction needs to be identified. Is it neurological? Is it mood disorder related? Is it related to psychological trauma? Is it a combination of some or all of the above? If so, which seems to be more predominant?

I have devised my own system of classification for those diagnosed with BPD. It is as follows:

BPD, Alpha Type: Symptoms actually ARE a type of an affective disorder, such as a variant of Bipolar II. I agree with Akisal, that this is really not BPD at all.

BPD, Beta Type: Symptoms actually ARE a type of Complex Post Traumatic Stress Disorder.
(Note: When this is true, many clinicians suggest that the BPD label is not appropriate for them anymore.)[43]

BPD, Gamma Type: I base the name of this type of the "Gamma Integration study" referenced earlier. Those of us who have primary neurological differences (such as autism, ADD or SID) would fit more properly as "Gamma" types.

I do not believe "gamma types" should be labeled as BPD either, since most of the reasons for meeting the BPD criteria are likely due to the primary neurological issues. Much more information about how to tell when this is true is included later in this chapter. Further research may show us that the vast majority of those patients identified as having BPD are actually "gamma" types. A 2006 review of 29 major studies, published in the Canadian Journal of Psychiatry showed the following result:

> Of the BPD studies, 83% found neuropsychological impairment in one or more cognitive domains, irrespective of depression, involving specific or generalized deficits linked to the dorsolateral prefrontal and orbitofrontal regions.[44]

The recent studies have consistently reflected more neurological involvement in BPD than was previously thought. This consensus in statistical data is far more compelling to me than any assertions that the phenomenon we have come to know as "BPD" is primarily either a mood or a trauma-based disorder. Also, this reflects that "BPD" is a disorder of neurology, rather than a disorder of character or personality.

If not, the "Gamma Type," may be the predominant type. 60-66% of BPD studies on neurological impairment with BPD also show significant visual-spatial and organizational problems.[45] Although 83% of studies show neurological deficits (as described above,) problems with visual-spatial areas specifically indicate right hemisphere brain dysfunction. Neurological deficits may even be the best predictor for the borderline personality diagnosis, rather than "mood lability."

I am not the first to come to this conclusion. Far more striking is how closely this 2006 study parallels a Canadian study conducted 13 years ago. It was postulated in 1993 by a team of researchers at McMaster University in Ontario, Canada that "an organic subgroup" of borderline personality might exist.

> The study found that 81% of the patients with BPD and 22% of the control patients had a history of brain injury, either developmental (44%), acquired (58%) or both. A pilot neuropsychological study showed that seven out of nine subjects with BPD (70%) showed evidence of frontal system dysfunction. These results help to support the hypothesized existence of an organic BPD subgroup.[46]

BPD, Delta Type: The "delta" designation is reserved for the most challenging cases of BPD. Delta, meaning "change," is most appropriate for those who fit into two or more of the above categories, and who are impossible to "peg" consistently. In this case, BPD might be an appropriate label. However, often a case like this will also have co-morbid DID (disocciative identity disorder,) which is an even better descriptive label.

The True Prognosis of
Borderline Personality Disorder

Good News!

* The borderline personality diagnosis has a better prognosis than for other serious mental illnesses, such as bipolar disorder.[47] [48] [49]
* Fortunately, most patients with BPD improve with time.[50] [51] [52]
* About 75% will regain close to normal functioning by the age of 35 to 40 years, and 90% will recover by the age of 50.[53]

Caveats

* Unfortunately, about 1 in 10 patients eventually succeeds in committing suicide.[54]
* However, this outcome is difficult to predict, and 90% of patients improve despite having threatened to end their lives on multiple occasions.[55]

In Summary

Proceeding from the root cause first in treatment strategy should result in the most dramatic decrease in borderline personality symptomology. For this reason, I agree with Perugi, Toni, Travierso and Akiskal that "the construct of borderline personality disorder is better covered by more conventional diagnostic entities."[56]

However, if you have been "tagged" with this label, it might be helpful for you to sort for yourself the same questions. What is your primary problem? Is it mood? Is it trauma? Is it brain functioning? Find the best assessment specialist you can find, and try to get a better description of your condition.

Based upon my analysis, the diagnosis "borderline personality disorder" says very little. So, you fit 5 of 9 criteria which are widely diverse and which could be more appropriately assigned to other diagnostic categories. So what? It's most important not to focus on that. Focus instead on what you, as a unique individual, need in order to get better.

The most important thing to remember is that you can recover. It does take dedicated effort, but hopefully some of the suggested guidelines in this book will help to make your recovery easier.

Overlooked Neurological Components that May Resemble BPD

Borderline symptoms may also be the result of chronic substance abuse and/or medical conditions (specifically, disorders of the central nervous system). These should be ruled out before making the diagnosis of borderline personality disorder.[57]

A 2006 Belgian article found added "evidence to the possibility of nonfocal CNS failure in BPD."[58] In May of 2005, I was diagnosed with "unspecified disorder of the autonomic nervous system." Newer diagnoses, more commonly assigned to school children, are now found to apply on a larger scale to adults.

Examples of these are Asperger's Disorder (1995,) and current psychological constructs such as Nonverbal Learning Disability (NLD) and Sensory Integration Disorder (SID). Older diagnoses, such as attention-deficit disorder (ADD) are now being applied to adults more often. None of the above-mentioned disabling conditions have any psychological origins. They result from patients who possess "different neurological wiring" for reasons unknown.

Non-Verbal Learning Disability (NLD or NVLD)

NLD is considered to be indicative of right-brain hemisphere dysfunction. Common within the context of Asperger's Syndrome, NLD is also a symptom or result of a wide variety of other neurological conditions. The dysfunction of NLD can result in grave difficulty with processing emotions, maintaining balance and coordination, movement in space, and understanding non-verbal communication. Tests revealed my visual-spatial memory on one test scored below the 1st percentile.

Finally, I understood my lifelong problems of chronically feeling lost and disoriented, and with having sudden, but transient attacks of panic or of other intense feelings that I could not process. I also understood for the first time why the children on the playground used to taunt me with "Laura is in La-La Land," and why people all my life have said to me, "You look lost." I used to analyze it and try to figure out why I was anxious and dissociated (i.e. spacing out due to trauma.) But, I wasn't. I may always "look lost" at times, but it really doesn't mean anything, other than I'm disoriented. The disorientation produces anxiety which has no psychological origin.

Professionals have suggested to me that anxiety may be either the sole cause or an exacerbating factor in how and why I "get lost" so often. However, when I have completed neuropsych testing, I've been calm and relaxed, but still unable to complete spatial tasks. I've also talked to many other people who were diagnosed with BPD and who also have had lifetime problems with maps, directions, and with the subtleties of non-verbal communication. I wonder if there is a pattern?

While there is not a direct relationship that may be generalized to everyone, in my case I believe it played a significant role in my development of the disorder, and these factors may also play a role in the etiology of how BPD develops for many people.

Wendy Heller, PhD outlines the developmental processes and dysfunction of the right hemisphere and its implications for learning and social perception in her article called *Understanding Non-Verbal Learning Disability.* She writes, "It is not unreasonable to expect that problems with processing the facial or prosodic information that goes along with parent-child interaction could result in a variety of detrimental outcomes for a child."

For so long, I grieved the lack of a sense of a bond with my mother. My brilliant, sensitive, powerful mother also showed many traits of NLD. I believe now that our combined right-hemisphere processing problems were what made our relationship the most difficult. So, receiving this diagnosis furthered my journey toward forgiveness, acceptance and release.

Dr. Wendy Heller continues, "Some authors have argued that deficits in right hemisphere functions may also interfere with the development of a cohesive sense of self. This could manifest in a variety of ways, depending on the severity of the problem."

In my case, I believe there was a strong relationship between NLD and BPD. It was never diagnosed when I was a child. Many of my "problem behaviors" were nothing more than my doing my best to interact socially when I couldn't comprehend the estimated 65-90% of conversation that non-verbal communication often makes up.

Still, today I have learned compensatory strategies to process non-verbal information. I do maintain a steady sense of who I am, through all the changes I experience. Many people who have been diagnosed with BPD who exhibit some of these symptoms I've described might want to consider getting a neuropsychological assessment to check for these underlying neurological conditions. I know it really opened my eyes.

The good news about coming to terms with NLD is that I will no longer allow myself to struggle unnecessarily in areas where I am not neurologically capable. However, I am now getting occupational therapy to help make my disability more manageable. I have realized that I need to let go of my independent spirit enough to ask for more help and support at times.

It will be impossible for me to wake up "instantly enlightened" and thus able to find my way across town and back without significant difficulty. Sometimes, getting through an ordinary day is exhausting for me, even after receiving treatment. So, it was a relief to realize that this is neurological, not psychological. Although I can not make my disability go away, there are ways that I can cope with it much better than I did before.

No matter how much I meditate and practice stress reduction, sometimes loud noises and unforeseen events will shake me up inside. Although I have accomplished much in my life, I will still work slowly to develop and strengthen weaker areas as much as I am able. Accepting my NLD (and my autistic condition in general) has helped me to empathize more deeply with a wide range of different neurological styles.

I don't believe they are disorders as much as "differences" which should be valued. In addition, because I was able to "get real," and let go of the "hidden shame" of my disability, I've been able to get a lot more constructive help with how to manage it.

Sensory Integration Disorder

Sensory Integration Disorder (SID) is a term coined by Jean Ayers, PhD, OTR. Occupational Therapists now often refer to it as Sensory Processing Disorder or SPD. Sensory integration dysfunction is "A neurological disorder characterized by disruption in the processing and organization of sensory information by the central nervous system, characterized by impaired sensitivity to sensory input, motor control problems, unusually high or low activity levels, and emotional instability." [59] In other words, in many cases, one of the "core" diagnostic criterion for BPD, emotional instability, may not be due to personality disorder at all.

> Cognitive distortions of BPD suggest lack of initial sensory integration, which may be a distinct deficit underlying differences with higher order cognition within this disorder.

-Leanne Williams, Sidis, Grodon, Meas, Sydney, NSW, Australia[60]

According to the KIDS foundation SPD network, "children with Sensory Processing Disorder (SPD) may suffer from behavioral problems. They may have problems with motor skills and other skills needed for school success. They may also be socially isolated and suffer from low self-esteem. Often they get a reputation for being a "difficult child."[61]

These difficulties put these children at high risk for many emotional, social, and educational problems, including the inability to make friends or be a part of a group, a poor self-concept, academic failure, and being labeled as clumsy, uncooperative, belligerent, disruptive, or out of control. Parents may be blamed for their children's behavior by people who are unaware of this "hidden handicap."

Factors that contribute to SID include: premature birth; **autism** and other developmental disorders; learning disabilities; delinquency and substance abuse due to learning disabilities; **stress-related disorders**; and brain injury. Two of the biggest contributing conditions are autism and attention-deficit hyperactivity disorder (**ADHD**).[62]

Sharon Heller echoes my sentiment and primary thesis best with this passage:

Loneliness, anxiety, extreme fatigue, sleep problems and lack of human affection set up depression, as does learned helplessness, the passive resignation that what you go for you don't get, so why bother. And the extreme stress associated with sensory defensiveness depletes serotonin. Marked shifts in mood, impulsive and unpredictable behavior, and great difficulty in personal relationships , which are often transitory, have earned many sensory-defensives the diagnosis of borderline personality.

(Sharon Heller, PhD is the author of *Too Loud, Too Bright, Too Fast Too Tight: What to do if you are Sensory Defensive in an Overstimulating World).*[63]

I also believe it is important to point out that when a patient is suffering from sensory issues and is complaining about the impact they are making on life, it is crucial that professionals NOT accuse the patient of taking a "victim position" towards life. Everyday living can traumatize those with sensory issues. This is a reality that should not be negated. Skills should be taught to help alleviate the discomfort and help the patient to cope more effectively.

Attention-Deficit Disorder and
Autism Spectrum Disorders

Boys and men are diagnosed with both autism spectrum disorders and attention deficit disorder at a 3:1 ratio to women and girls. The reverse ratio is true for borderline personality disorder. 75-80% of those diagnosed with BPD are women. Is there a bias towards women having more "psychological issues," vs. men who have more "neurologically based" issues?

When a male patient enters a psych unit in a regressed state, self-injuring and prone to outbursts, most clinicians think in terms of the more frequent male diagnoses outlined above. When a female patient enters a psych unit in a regressed state, self-injuring and prone to outbursts, the immediate clinical diagnosis that comes to mind is "borderline personality disorder," especially if she happens to be carrying a teddy bear and is a frequent "cutter."

"Attention Deficit Disorder Hits Women Harder," says a May, 2005 article by Paula Moyer, published on Med Page Today, and covered by Fox news:

> Their symptoms tend to be more severe, and they live with more emotional impairment than do male patients, according to Fred W. Reimherr, M.D., of the University of Utah in Salt Lake City, and colleagues who presented their findings at American Psychiatric Association meeting here this week. [64]

Attention-deficit disorder is likely to be under-diagnosed in women, along with autism spectrum disorders. Women with Asperger's Syndrome (AS) present very differently than boys and men. Women with AS tend to be more imaginative than men. They also display more compassion and empathy. [65]Emotional impairment and moodiness may be more common with autism spectrum disorders in women than they are in men.

In their book, *Driven to Distraction*, authors Edward Hallowell, M.D. and John Ratey, M.D [66]outline several interesting points of intersection that BPD has with ADD. Both conditions share these traits: Impulsivity is common; substance abuse is not uncommon; mood instability and underachievement are all shared in both conditions.

They state that someone with BPD has a "poorly formed inner self," but someone with ADD has a "distracted inner self."[67] The authors don't seem to describe this difference with much specific depth, but it is clear that these two processes are very different. Identifying which process is going on can make the essential difference in which medication treatment will be the most effective. During the process of clinical interviewing, many professionals immediately jump to the conclusion that it "must be BPD," without more carefully analyzing patterns of behavior and cognition.

Both people with BPD and people who have ADD use external axes to organize themselves internally. Both require and appreciate organizing structures in their environment, and they both need structure in their lives far more than most people do. People with ADD use "high stimulation" to organize themselves.

High stimulation situations help them to focus, which paradoxically results in a sense of calm and relaxation. BPD sufferers also use "high stimulation," but the purpose is to ease pain, rather than to organize their personalities. A commonality is how the axes both ADD and BPD people use to organize themselves tend to involve the search for structure and purpose, in order to quell the anxiety caused by internal disorganization.

The authors further state that "one of the primary feelings of the borderline syndrome is rage, "which can come clawing out unpredictably and apparently unprovoked." However, both ADD and BPD sufferers share the anger characteristic, but in response to different things. BPD sufferers react to unmet needs. ADD sufferers react with frustration over their inconsistent performance.

Another similarity is how borderline individuals are also "exquisitely sensitive to rejection," while people with ADD are also "easily hurt and rejected." The ADD individual "tunes out" in relationships, while the authors describe how the BPD individual will often abruptly end relationships due to the fear of intimacy.

The authors did not point out how people suffering from BPD also tune out in relationships. This is often due to dissociation (i.e. "spacing out" due to traumatic stress triggers OR from sensory overload). In most cases, people with BPD will cling to relationships, refusing to admit they are over, long after their partner has separated from them. This dynamic may be created from "abandonment anxiety."

According to Drs. Halloway and Ratey, the prevalence of ADD is higher among foster children and adopted children than it is in the general population. The authors suggest that this may be because of neurological damage caused by early life in poverty or having a drug-addicted mother.

Rather, it is possible that even in wealthy homes that provide a healthy physical environment, parental neglect often occurs. When this happens, neurological damage may also result. Although this is true, evidence that ADD is genetic, rather than environmental, is far more compelling.[68]

The authors offer the example of two children who were adopted and who developed "out of control," ADHD appearing behavior. The school staff of a special nursery school believed that the children had problems because of "unconscious, repressed feelings about their biological mother."

However, the adopted parents had consistently conveyed the message to the children that their mother loved them, wanted them, fought for them, and was very unhappy that she was unable to care for them. When the children were removed from this school and placed in public school, the school counselor suspected ADD was the problem.

Upon assessment, severe ADD was assessed in both children, and medication treatment completely corrected their problems. Drs. Halloway and Ratey give this example to show the significance of proper diagnosis. As they say, "How dangerous and damaging would it have been if these boys had never been treated for the right condition?"

This example led me to wonder whether the concept of "abandonment" is often planted in the minds of psychiatric patients. I can remember, in my early days of therapy, being asked questions such as, "Did you every feel abandoned?" If I said "No," the question became, "What about emotionally? Were your parents distant?" My answer to this question would easily be, "Yes." Why were these questions asked, anyway? Maybe the clinician was checking to see whether I met a diagnostic criterion for BPD.

I have never read any literature regarding successful treatment for abandonment trauma. Once, I believed I had developed the answer, and had written it, in the previous version of this book. I believed that because for many years, I had no thoughts or feelings related towards resenting my parents for not being available to me. I had used techniques that really did help me to feel that I had "healed the abandonment wound" completely. They helped a great deal. They have helped many other people equally. I'm not sure that the feeling of abandonment will never recur.

Within the last year, I've felt occasionally a very sad and anxious feeling, grieving that my mother seemed to reject me quite often. Does this mean I have failed at healing from Criterion #2? What if I have not? What if this simply cannot be done? Well, then obviously, myself and all patients diagnosed with BPD must remain on Axis II, personality disordered for the rest of their lives. At least, that's how it might appear to the creators of the Diagnostic and Statistical Manual for Mental Disorders. That is their decision. My decision is to grieve it, move on and stop trying to heal from this proposed "abandonment thing."

If parents were distant and neglectful for any reason, whether it be due to their extended physical or mental illness, death or spending excessive time away from home, it is very possible that the neurological development of children could be affected. We know that no therapeutic technique so far has helped to resolve "abandonment issues," and yet therapists persist in bringing them up and attempting resolution.

Why not fully assess and treat the neurological damage that has been created as a result, rather than encouraging patients (including small children like these in the story) to develop unnecessary resentments towards their absent parents?

When I read this, I started to ask myself, "When was the first time I believed I was abandoned?" I actually had to think a long time about this subject, because it was hard for me to remember any concrete examples. I remember experiences of my mother's rejection, from a very early age. But, the sense of abandonment did not occur until my mid-twenties. Finally, it occurred to me exactly at which point of time I began to identify with this construct.

The identification began during my inappropriately sexual three year relationship with my treating psychologist. He had convinced me that I needed him and had to depend on him. So, after that, when he left, I felt abandonment feelings. I don't remember feeling those particular feelings before that time.

When I had initially identified with the criteria for BPD in graduate school, it was not because of abandonment fear. It was because I related to having a sense of an incomplete self that I was trying to fill up through any means I could. Of course, I could not have realized at that time that I may have merely had a "distracted self." This concept had never been presented to me in graduate school.

I grew to "organize myself" under the construct of borderline personality disorder during that time, and the psychologist I lived with consistently (and for an extended period of duration) treated me within this context, until this became who I believed that I was.

Ten years later, I began to "organize myself" within the construct of Asperger's Syndrome. So many aspects of my early childhood seemed consistent with this diagnosis, including my extreme hyperlexia, motor clumsiness, lack of coordination, and lack of ability to form friendships. I also had the usual, related passionate and obsessive interests. Living with Asperger's Syndrome is exponentially more difficult than living with only ADD. However, parents and teachers may notice that severe ADD impairs students almost as much as AS in terms of getting schoolwork completed and turned in on time.

Using ADD as an organizing structure was helpful to me and it fit better than any other diagnosis so far. I would never have considered it. I believed only misbehaving boys with bad grades had that, not bright, daydreaming girls who still made straight A's. At that time, examining my life within an ADD paradigm actually fit me better than any other framework I had considered so far. Still, the most expert assessor whom I consulted was uncertain regarding the ADD diagnosis for me. To him, the argument to view those symptoms as a part of my autism was "more profound and compelling."

With my deficits being treated, I felt like a cloud lifted. I could not believe I had lived my entire life walking in a fog. Gradually, I became more able to choose when to daydream and when not to, although at the moment, I sometimes will space out and require more support and re-direction when I'm very tired or over-stressed. Prioritizing challenges me. I also seem to have almost no sense whatsoever of chronological time!

One aspect of my focusing that has not changed is this: When I am immersed in something that fascinates me, I am completely unaware of time, space or anything but what I am experiencing. I'm not sure that I want this part of my personality to change. This is one of the aspects of my autism I love the most. I love to "dive in" and fully immerse myself in my subjects of interest.

People with ADD (and people who have Asperger's Syndrome) will often organize their thoughts around hyper-focused negativity. Since I primarily use a hyper-focused mode in my style of ADD (which has many OCD traits,) I was frustrated for years that my mind could still slip into these patterns under stress, regardless of how much meditation or active fighting back with coping skills I used.

Finally, I learned that this is a neurological problem that just happens automatically. It is sometimes called "thought looping." Trying to stop doing this sort of thing without medication would be like trying to stop your heart from beating with your thoughts. Maybe an accomplished yogi could.   I could not, although I worked very hard at this goal and periodically believed I had permanently eliminated it!

With increased freedom from thought-looping, I began to have a lot more fun with the idea that my choices are what create my identity. I became able to make some of the choices I was unable make in the past. The decision to take medications was not a failure of will. Anyone who knows me well will testify to my sustained commitment to recovery. The truth difficult for me to accept is that when neurological functioning is impaired, choices are more limited. Today, I have a brain that functions much better than it ever has before. Because of this, I am creating an entirely new life. More choices have opened up as the result of having clearer and more functional brain pathways for decision processing to flow through.

Added Note:
In Appendix I, I provide a chart that outlines the similarities and differences between borderline presonality disorder and autism spectrum disorders. I made many surprising discoveries through doing my research. I present the facts. You may draw your own conclusions!

In conclusion...

No other psychiatric diagnosis appears quite so vague and so easily confused with other disorders as borderline personality disorder. Moreover, people who are diagnosed with this disorder are generally miserable people who live lives completely out of control. Most spend quite a long time in denial of their condition. After they are aware that they may be suffering from an unhealthy psychological condition, they launch into blaming other people and "victim-thinking" quite a lot.

Some of this, I believe, is actually encouraged by therapists who focus too intensively on "abandonment issues," especially when the patient hasn't brought them up in the first place. In no way do I discredit the truth that some patients are aware that they have been deeply hurt through a sense of abandonment, and their feelings need a safe place to be heard and processed.

Anger is also an essential part of the healing process. All people need permission and a safe place to express their anger regarding unmet needs and past traumas. Yet, eventually, with proper motivational support, mentally ill persons can start to realize that if they take responsibility for their life choices, they have the potential to get better and lead more fulfilling lives.

Admitting that there IS a problem is often more important than having the exactly correct "clinical label" for what that problem is. In my own case, I had to admit that my core problem was the inability to take responsibility for myself. Nine years following my decision to dedicate myself to being responsible, I underwent the painful process of admitting I could not do it all "on my own," because the framework of my problem was not some vague, amorphous psychological construct. Instead, it was a solid, neurological difference in brain structure and functioning. Saying, "I need help," turned out to be a lot more important than arriving at my ultimate diagnostic label. During this year, all of my therapy has been helpful.

Without exception, each clinician who has reviewed my past history has agreed that I did meet the criteria for borderline personality disorder during the years I described. Also, for the time being, borderline personality disorder exists as an officially recognized diagnostic entity. Therefore, I address suffering from this condition by referring to BPD as if it is truly a credible disorder. I refer to its standard clinical presentation, treatment options, and coping skills.

Although I write according to the established and traditional guidelines for 2006, I must admit that my extensive research on the subject has called into question whether borderline personality disorder really exists. I am not alone. Many professionals feel the same way. I do not know whether I ever had BPD, ever recovered from it or have ever known anyone who has had it or recovered from it.

All I definitely know at this point in time is that if you have been diagnosed with this disorder, (or any of the related conditions I have delineated which overlap with it significantly,) you may find many of the techniques in this book helpful. They will guide you in practicing how to make life choices that allow you to define who you are.

THE

BORDERLINE

AND BEYOND

PROGRAM

What IS the "Borderline and Beyond Program"?

Borderline and Beyond is more than a book. It is a program of recovery. It is a method of self-realization, an aid in personal reflection, and a stimulus to growth and healing. *Borderline and Beyond* is intended to inform you about some of the features of borderline personality disorder (BPD) and the treatment available, both through professional and self-help resources. You will learn more about this disorder and what is known by professionals about how to treat it. If you have been given a different, yet related psychiatric diagnosis, you will also find yourself "at home" with the information and resources provided herein.

The *Borderline and Beyond Workbook*, which is now available separately, contains journal pages that are structured so that you can get the maximum psychological benefit through the exercise of writing. There are tests along the way, which you can use to monitor your progress. New blank journals are also available on the LauraPaxton.com web-site.

Hopefully, you will enjoy this experience of reading *Borderline and Beyond, Revised*, which has been made entertaining through the use of the allegory and metaphor so richly abundant in stories, fables, poetry and critiques of movies and novels. In addition, you will get more in touch with your own creative powers and abilities, and learn to trust your own intuition and creativity to begin your own healing process.

My hope is that you will come away from this experience with a veritable arsenal of coping skills to use when confronted by stressors. My hope is that your knowledge of yourself, your illness, and your hope for the future will all increase, and that this book will have comforted and supported you every step of the way. Believe with me that there is life beyond borderline personality disorder and that through working this program, you can discover what that means to you.

What This Book Is Not

- The Expanded 2007 Edition is currently **not intended only for sufferers of "BPD."** This book is now intended for any person struggling with "black and white conceptualization of the world," intense emotional experiences, struggles with personal identity, and any of the other various traits of BPD, many of which may be better attributed to another disorder. **Examples:** Autism Spectrum Disorders, Attention Deficit Disorder, Sensory Integration Disorder, Bipolar Disorder, Post Traumatic Stress Disorder
- This book was originally intended for persons already diagnosed with borderline personality disorder by a mental health professional. **This program will not diagnose whether or not you are suffering from borderline personality disorder.** Such a diagnosis will need to be made by a mental health professional who has met with you face to face.
- This program is **not a magic cure** for borderline personality disorder or any other syndrome or disorder. In order for this program to produce results in your life, you must work to the best of your ability on a regular basis in the workbook or in a personal journal.
- This book is **not a substitute for psycho-therapy** or a consultation with a mental health professional.
- This program is **not going to prevent you from facing stresses and struggles in your**

daily life. It will only help you to cope with them better.

- Following the suggestions of this book **does not guarantee that you will have no more "borderline episodes."** This program is to be a companion in the healing process, to help you get through times of crisis. Working this program can help you get focused more quickly after an episode of "borderline" symptoms.
- Not all of the information contained in this book will relate to every individual case of "borderline personality." **It's possible for those diagnosed with borderline personality disorder to have some, but not all of the features and symptoms mentioned in this book.**
- Also keep in mind that the diagnosis of BPD that you bear **may or may not be an accurate description of you and your behavior.** Other diagnostic possibilities may need to be explored instead, so that you may find more effective treatment.

About the Overall Process

None of the material in this program is intended to be read only once and then forgotten. It is intended to be re-read and worked through as often as necessary. The original version of *Borderline and Beyond* was a combination workbook, journal and text. This version of *Borderline and Beyond* is text only, but another workbook is now available. I also suggest using a journal when you feel agitated, angry, empty or depressed.

Although you should first call a mental health professional immediately, if you feel like harming yourself or someone else, when you are upset and free from danger, journal your feelings and ideas. Journaling offers an outlet to express your pain without acting on it in a harmful way.

Let the work itself be an alternative to negative coping. Let the work itself be a comfort to you in times of crisis. If you wish, use this program as a "transitional object," as you would use a favorite blanket, photograph, or even a stuffed toy. Sometimes, certain objects (such as those described above) remind us of our relationships to people who are away. Associate this program with comfort, hope, structure, guidance, nurturance and for the fulfillment needs for self-expression. Turn to it rather than to self-harm in its many forms and you will eventually find that you are miraculously turning to yourself. This process is part of an amazing journey of self-discovery.

The type of work you do in the *Borderline and Beyond Workbook* is varied. It ranges from checklists to questions which provoke deep thought to games or play and exercises to perform to strengthen your skills in self-comforting and emotional modulation. The work also includes creative activities such as drawing and writing. Anything you feel uncomfortable with may be skipped, but no one needs to look at your work except for you and your therapist, if you choose to share your work with your therapist.

This program is best utilized in tandem with therapy. Sharing your work with a therapist will strengthen progress and insight far more than merely working on the exercises by yourself. Remember that recovery is a very "up and down" process. Do not be discouraged if after a few good days you have a series of bad ones. This is just the nature of the condition we have come to know as "borderline personality disorder."

This is also the nature of autism spectrum disorders. Preparing for the possibility of an "emotional meltdown" minimizes the intensity when meltdowns arise. Sometimes, preparation helps to avoid them completely. However, meltdowns are a part of life.

Whatever the obstacle, continue to trudge forward in your recovery. Sometimes, you are learning more than you realize. The important thing is to continue trying, no matter what. Good luck to you and "Bon Voyage" as you begin your journey into better mental health and a more hope-filled future.

Note: About the Gender Used In the Text

Few studies have been done about gender differences and how they impact clinical presentation and course of treatment. Zlotnick and Zimmerman's 2002 study reflected that no gender differences impacted overall impairment.[69] However, a 2003 study showed that men diagnosed with BPD were more likely to also receive such diagnoses as antisocial personality disorder, intermittent explosive disorder, and substance abuse disorder. Women developed more eating disorders than the men in the study.[70]

When referring to the borderline patient by use of pronouns, I have opted in most cases to use "her" and "she" as opposed to "he" or "him." This is because there are currently more female patients being diagnosed with this disorder. This in no way implies that there are more women who have borderline personality disorder, nor does it indicate a gender bias on my part. I am simply using the female gender because I am directing my terminology to the majority of the population currently diagnosed with this disorder.

Step One
How to Make a Commitment to Your Recovery

Some illnesses are considered possible to recover from, while others are considered "impossible." For example, mental retardation and autism are considered "impossible" to recover from. One can improve and learn to cope with the different neurological wiring of autism, yet still the fundamental structure of the brain is different.

"Borderline personality disorder" used to be considered "impossible" to recover from. However, the past decade of research has shown that recovery is not only possible, but it is the usual course of outcome for those originally labeled with BPD. By one's mid to late 30's, commonly only a few (if any,) traits of this "disorder" remain.

Psychiatrists place illnesses considered "impossible" to recover from on Axis II of the current five axis diagnostic structure. However, not everyone recovers from this diagnostic construct that we have come to know as "BPD." One in every ten people with this diagnosis die of suicide. This rate is higher than for those diagnosed with major depression.

There is a strong movement to rename BPD and move it to Axis I. So, if you want to recover from "borderline personality disorder," (OR learn to live with a developmental, neurological difference,) the most important question to ask yourself is, "What do I believe?" Are you able to believe in your own power to recover? It takes an incredible amount of commitment, energy and work to recover from any severe emotional or neurological illness. Why aren't more people committed to the process? Having a commitment to your self requires a certain amount of self-love to begin with. If you don't love yourself, why would you commit to putting energy toward your greatest benefit? If a mother doesn't love her baby, will she feed it and support it?

More people aren't committed to the process of recovery from severe emotional disorders because they don't realize that they are worth it. In addition to not having much of a sense of inner worth, the person diagnosed with BPD feels weighted down with powerful emotions, such as rage or depression. The frustration of seeking help and not experiencing effective treatment (i.e. treatment that relieves symptoms) adds to the overall sense of hopelessness, and helplessness. She focuses on these negative emotions, giving them even more power and energy over her. Very little energy is left over to begin to think positively and to change her life.

One of the best ways to start the process of recovery is to make the agreement that you will no longer speak out negatively about yourself, and that you won't believe any negative things about yourself. Don't put yourself down, and don't take seriously any thoughts that say that you cannot recover from borderline personality disorder or improve your life. Even if a doctor or other professionals speak to you in a negative way about your prognosis, do not believe them. You need all the energy you have to recover, so you cannot afford to waste your energy believing in negative things.

Commitment to being responsible for yourself must come first, above all else. Without it, you cannot recover. To strengthen your commitment, or "will," cultivate the practice of recognizing when you are telling yourself negative stories and don't believe them. Don't judge yourself for thinking negatively, but realize that you have a choice and can stop feeding negativity. Put all your energy in the direction of loving yourself, and you can recover.

When I began my recovery process from BPD, it was because I finally gave up that anyone else could help me. I realized that my choice was to fully commit myself to doing everything in my power to recover or to die. My suicide attempts had always been thwarted, so that I ended up alive and miserable each time I swallowed a bottle of pills.

Although I was hospitalized a total of eleven times in my lifetime, six hospitalizations occurred in one year. My last suicide attempt was in October of 1996, before the final hospitalization. After I survived what I believed would be fatal overdose, I decided that if I had to live on this earth, I would have to put all of my available energy into recovery.

I prayed a lot during that time, and I asked for God to "show me what love is" and to "open up a way to heal." Both of those prayers have been answered for me. I believe that in times of extreme stress, if we open ourselves up to it, our body and soul have a natural ability to heal. I am a strong believer in the power of prayer and in the power of God, because I have experienced that power working in my own life and in the lives of others. We must pray for God to open this natural ability to us, to make us receptive to it.

That is why, when deciding whether or not to make a commitment to your recovery process, it is important to ask yourself, "What do I believe?" You can't make any change in your life until you first believe it is possible. What you choose to believe controls where you decide to put your energy. If you want to recover, you need all of the energy you can get, dedicated towards healing yourself and your life. You cannot afford to waste any energy at all indulging in feeling like a victim of life circumstances. You need to believe in your own power and in the power of God with all of your might.

If you put all of your energy in the direction of loving yourself, your relationships with others will improve. This is because we automatically treat other people the way we treat ourselves. Our outer relationships reflect our relationship with ourselves.

When we love ourselves fully, we stop expecting and demanding other people to fulfill functions for us that we believe we cannot fulfill. It is selfish to expect someone else to love us in ways that we cannot love ourselves. Another person will not be able to do it, and both of us will be resentful.

Many therapists believe that people suffering from BPD have "developmental deficits" that can only be filled by spending years in therapy, learning to internalize the structuring, nurturing and supportive functions of the therapist. These deficits stem from unfulfilled needs in childhood. Although this approach may be helpful, if you are able to commit yourself to the process of changing your usual habits in regard to other people, you will expedite the process of strengthening your sense of inner self.

Simply begin consciously to notice when you have expectations that others should provide a need for you, or when you experience longing and an empty feeling of desperation and emptiness. Instead develop the discipline to look within yourself for support and love. Realize that who you are is defined by your ability to make your own choices. You are defined by what you do, not by what you feel. Following this basic practice will eventually result in lasting change.

Your therapist can help, but people with borderline personality disorder tend to become over-dependent on the therapist. The more your therapist deflects responsibility back to you, the more certain it is that you will begin to heal The most important element of "BPD" recovery is this: Make the strong and solid commitment to loving yourself, no matter what. I encourage you to write out that commitment now.

Step Two:
How to Make Choices
When Feeling Incomplete or Even Crazy

In the opening scene from the movie *Edward Scissorhands*, an Avon lady stumbles upon a Gothic castle, back in the woods from her quiet suburban neighborhood. As unrealistic as this seems, she finds a young man kneeling in the corner of an attic. He stands, revealing two large pairs of scissors where his hands should be. Noticing her shocked reaction, he states, "I'm not finished yet."

As we later discover in the movie, he was being created by a scientist who died before he could finish Edward's hands. Angry, bereaved and bitter, Edward could have used these "scissor hands" for any malevolent purpose, ripping and tearing into any person crossing his path, or even into himself in confusion and disgust with himself. Yet, Edward does not. He uses his hands to create beautiful sculptures out of wood, shrubbery, ice, and even hair. Even though the story has a tragic ending, Edward has transformed his handicap into an instrument of beauty.

So it can be with the "borderline," and sometimes, the autistic. She, too, is "not finished yet," due to developmental arrest (or delay,) and she is trying to hide this fact from the world. Instead of capable hands to care for and nurture herself, she has the sharp instruments of self-hatred and frustration constantly at her disposal. Not automatically able to transform the negative to positive, she is always cutting and tearing into herself and into others with hands meant to reach out for love and nurturance. She has not learned how to transform her handicap into a beautiful thing. By looking at case studies or by examining the person you know with BPD intimately, you can clearly see how this transformation is not easy to undertake.

Neither was the awesome transformation of Edward easy to attain. Of course, the movie was only a fairy tale. Or was it? What we can believe, we often have the power to manifest. However, belief must come first.

What are the possible strengths evident in the borderline condition? People diagnosed with BPD are sometimes prone to "micro-psychotic episodes," or short-lived flights from reality. The state of psychosis itself has been associated with the primitive mind, the childlike mind, or the wild mind.

From this source come the very origins of creativity and intuition. The borderline, unlike the pure psychotic, can dip in and out of these states, for brief intervals, although at uncontrolled times. Creative thinking should be a natural by-product if art or poetry or music is used to sort out the chaos within. Using art as an aid to cohesion and integration has been a survival tool for many persons afflicted with the borderline syndrome.

It has been said that where there is breath there is hope. Within each person, regardless of health, there is a drive toward getting better and improving, and a drive toward destructiveness. The latter drive, of course, is stronger in the borderline condition, which makes it all the more important to fight these urges by using art as a means of cohesion. The fragility of the borderline lessens when her energies are channeled in a positive direction. It is possible to live productively when one is "not finished yet." It is possible to live creatively and successfully when one has "scissors for hands."

The following are examples of poems that were used to communicate emotional pain, in order to deal with it creatively, instead of reactively:

Wounding

Wounding
Feels like illusion,
And I hold on to the pain.
The way you held my body there,
My Pain, My Comfort, my Despair,
I cry, I scream, I feel alive,
My soul has left my pleading eyes.
I cry, I scream, and I hate you
Rock me softly, cut right through.
This is a sacrifice for hope;
Another martyrdom for hope,
As my healing feels like illusion
And I lose my grip to cope.

Feeling Needy

I've got the hollow aching feeling
creeping through me again,
All the empty spaces biting through my skin.
I'm looking at you with needy eyes.
Can I borrow your confident walk or disguise?
You look like someone who could organize my mind
and pour some medicine into the spaces inside
and I salivate with starving eyes
because I lack the strength that you provide.
I need a reassurance I.V.,
I need a soul-structure splint,
I need a comforting bubble to keep out the world's
debris.
I need an angel, please God to take away my misery.
I've got that hollow aching feeling
creeping deep in my skin
It hurts so bad with all its screaming needs again
I want to make it stop and shut it up with more pain
because I can't have what I need and it drives me
insane.

EXPANDED APPLICATIONS:
For those with BPD or on the Autistic Spectrum/ related disorders, such as NLD, ADD, and SPD:

Ten years ago, when I wrote the section above, I was not aware of the many articles on-line that describe the Edward Scissorhands character as a metaphor for Asperger's Disorder. Many of these reasons are the same reasons I chose Edward as a metaphor for BPD. He is socially awkward. He is very uncomfortable around others. He has the sense of "incompleteness," but also he uses his handicap in what could be considered an obsessive or perseverative way. As he creates art with his "scissor hands," he is communicating in the only way he knows how.

Very recently, I read an article about Tim Burton, producer and creator of both Edward Scissorhands and The Corpse Bride. This article described how closely Burton himself identifies with the deep, concentrated focus held by those with Asperger's Syndrome.[71]

Again, regardless of how you have been diagnosed, the lessons are the same. Edward Scissorhands is a great fictional role-model for how to convert "disability" into "strength." He also shows how he was able to find his own way to communicate in positive ways, despite his great difficulties.

Many people diagnosed with the neurological conditions above sometimes self-injure. Incidentally, self-injury is no longer an automatic "marker" for either BPD or autism. A recent study showed that one out of every 5 college students (20%) are currently self-injuring.[72] It is clear that not all of these are "borderline," since the rate of BPD is only estimated to include 1-3% of the general population. The rate of those diagnosed with autism spectrum disorders is under 1%, but the majority do not attend college.

No Self-Harm Contract:

Sign this contract about what you will do if the urge to hurt yourself strikes:

I _____ agree not to inflict bodily injury or pain upon myself. If I feel the urge coming on to do so, I will contact _____ or _____ (two names) and talk about how I am feeling. I will use these coping skills so that I will not engage in self harm:

(1)

(2)

I care about myself enough to take these steps to keep myself safe.

Signed,

Date: ___ / ___ / ___

"Borderline" Sexuality vs. Self-Injurious Behavior

The literature regarding people diagnosed with BPD and sexuality has focused upon a variety of "deviant" sexual behavior styles, often shown by people diagnosed with BPD. For example, some researchers have noticed the commonness of multiple paraphilias or fetishes, or a predominance of homosexual or bisexual urges.[73]

I have begun to wondered over the past few years whether or not this behavior has been unfairly pathologized. Certain types of sexual behavior are truly deviant and should be discouraged and criminally prosecuted, including sex with children or unwilling participants. However, could a proclivity toward many different styles of sexual expression merely indicate creativity?

The main lesson I have learned over the past few years has been that acceptance is the key to healing. I have come to recognize unconditional love is a sort of "universal medicine." This certainly extends to the approach we take to our own sexuality.

Acceptance of all of our sexual urges is paramount to recovery, whether we choose to act on them or not. We cannot heal and grow when we reject any part of ourselves. I have also learned that the more people accept their sexuality, the less likely they are to engage in obsessive thinking or compulsive behavior regarding it.

Often, patients diagnosed with borderline personality disorder have masochistic sexual fetishes. If a person is aroused by masochistic sex, this is a matter of personal sexual style. This usually has nothing whatsoever to do with self mutilation or self-injurious behavior in a borderline sense. These are completely different things. Mildly masochistic fetish behavior bears little resemblance to carving into one's arm with a knife in order to deal with feelings of overwhelming emotional anguish.

Sensory Integration Disorder is often the root cause of fetish behaviors involving bondage, heavy pressure or pain. Because the sensory processing system is different, sometimes heavier pressure (or what might be perceived as "pain" to someone else) is the only way to "register" the sense of touch. Treatment can relieve symptoms. Methods such as the Wilbarger Brushing Protocol have been researched extensively and found to be very helpful with tactile processing problems in many situations.

However, people diagnosed with borderline personality still need to look at whether they are using any form of sex to avoid facing their own needs for healing. People who rely on fetish behavior in a sexual sense may need to look at their own beliefs regarding their bodies. They need to ask themselves whether or not this behavior truly honors the temple of the divine that is their body.

For clinicians, assessment of the level of risk or potential danger involved in a sexual encounter is also paramount. Many people come to be diagnosed with BPD due in part to their proclivity for dangerous or risky sex. Through psychotherapy, many of these issues can be worked through so that these behaviors occur less often or not at all.

Step Three:
Making Choices
When It's Hard to Accept Adult Life

The following vignette illustrates the experience many people with have when they realize the damaging impact that BPD or a developmental disability has had on their lives:

> "Mommy, I just had a really bad dream. I dreamed that I grew up and never had a happy marriage and couldn't find a job that I could handle real well and I had to go into a hospital repeatedly over the course of my life because my feelings hurt so bad I wanted to die. Bad things kept happening over and over and it seemed like years before I woke up."
> "This was no dream, dear. It is reality. All those years have flown by and you're still four years old inside, so you never could manage your life the way you wanted to. You have been frozen in time and the ice is barely breaking."
> "When it melts, will I be four again and get to start over?"
> "No, you have to stay around and face each painful day patiently. It's the only way."
> "In the mean time, how do I ease the pain?"

Negative Ways To Cope:

Drugs & Alcohol
Self-Mutilation
Abusive Relationships
Suicide
Nervous Eating
Sexual Escapades
Impulsive Decisions
Dangerous Behaviors

Compulsive Shopping
Compulsive Gambling

Positive Ways to Cope:

Hug a teddy bear
Draw a picture
Write a poem
Do a craft project
Listen to music
See a movie
Take a walk
Call a friend
Read a book
Exercise
Take a nap
Meditate/Pray

Can you actually "go back in time" and be four again? Physically you can't. Spiritually you can. You can return to the same happiness, wild imagination and freedom you experienced as a child. However, you will need to do it with the wisdom of an adult, with the strong presence of a well-built internal observer, or "witness." This is a primary goal of the "mindfulness training" so often recommended as a component of treatment for BPD.

When you master the ability to observe yourself non-judgmentally, you can provide a loving, safe container for your inner child to feel safe to explore and enjoy life. However, sometimes, the pain feels too intense to contain. In the very beginning stages, it is helpful to know how to cope with overwhelming feelings, so that you do not allow them not to drown you.

How to Cope When Feelings Overwhelm You:

1. Place both feet on the ground and breathe slowly and deeply, being as aware as you can be of sights and sounds in your environment.
2. Repeat the year and date to yourself over and over.
3. Tag each finger of your hand with an emotion you are feeling. For example, your thumb is abandonment, your ring finger is anger, middle finger fear, etc. Hold each finger one by one and breathe deeply to soothe yourself and let the feeling go.
4. Distract your mind. Count backwards, try to say the alphabet backwards. Try to remember the names of the presidents or the colors of the rainbow.
5. Try a structured meditation game. One of my favorites is to think of one thing you are grateful for, one thing you need right now, one thing you hope for in the future, and then a word that expresses how you feel. Write a poem or word that seems to calm you down when you think of it. Then go back and repeat, only think of two things for each category, then three, until you feel yourself calm down.
6. Some psychiatrists prescribe non-addictive drugs that can calm you down when you are re-living abandonment trauma and get so upset that you can not calm down on your own. Ask your doctor.

Most importantly, ANY time you are feeling suicidal, call your doctor or therapist. You may already be too upset to calm down on your own and see suicide as the only answer.

Problems & Solutions:

When the problem is trust...
You are feeling afraid to talk to anyone.
You may cancel plans with people.
You might not leave the house for days.
You feel scared and anxious most of the time.
Nothing seems to comfort you.

...treat yourself like a colicky baby

> Follow grounding/calming down suggestions listed on the previous page.
> Try rocking, holding a stuffed toy, napping.
> Force yourself to talk to someone.
> Tell yourself, "I'm feeling too scared to have anybody around, but I know some company would help."

When the problem is control...
You are scared of losing control.
You are afraid of going crazy or hurting yourself.
You are testing people around you to see if they care about you.
You want to do things that are bad for you.
You feel guilty because you don't understand why you're doing what you do.

....treat yourself like a frustrated toddler

> Set a limit for yourself, like "I will not use the charge card.." Then, tell one other person or even enlist her help in holding on to the card for you for a while. Make a promise to that person. Think of something else you can do that would be positive. Structure your time. (Example: For the next thirty minutes, I will do laundry. For the next ten minutes, I will read a book.)

IF YOU ARE INTENSELY AFRAID YOU CAN'T CONTROL YOUR BEHAVIOR, LET SOMEONE KNOW IMMEDIATELY.

IF PLANS INVOLVE SELF-HARM OR SUICIDE, YOU NEED TO CALL A DOCTOR OR LICENSED MENTAL HEALTH PROFESSIONAL.

Step Four
How to Make Choices through
Learning Sensory Modulation Skills

Our sensory system serves as the primary source of our input from the external world. Because we perceive or process this stimuli differently, learning methods to modulate these responses is essential. For many years, autistic children have had the opportunity to experience these methods of "sensory modulation," via occupational therapy.

However, many people diagnosed with psychiatric illnesses only have the five secondary senses (taste, touch, seeing, hearing and smell) addressed within therapy that targets coping skill development. Without deeper work to modulate sensory experience, often methods of "emotional modulation" are not fully effective.

If you have been diagnosed with "borderline personality disorder," many methods employed by occupational therapists may prove very helpful to you. As Karen M Moore, MT, OTR/L's 1998 article explains, dialectical behavioral therapy (DBT) focuses well on ways to soothe the five basic senses (touch, taste, smell, hearing, sight,) but it does not also address vestibular of proprioceptic calming techniques.[74]

The vestibular system regulates our sense of balance and position in space. The proprioceptive system is the system that connects the mind to the body, so that fluid movements are possible. Techniques employed to modulate these deeper sensory functions provide far greater overall calming than targeting merely the five basic sensory systems. In Moore's article, "Sensory Based Therapy: The Missing Piece in DBT," she outlines how, when deeper vestibular and proprioceptic issues are addressed and treated, using OT techniques, deeper and more sustained sensory, and therefore emotional modulation occurs.

Occupational Therapy (OT) treatment is essential for treating sensory integration dysfunction (SID,) which I suffer from. One core component of SID is "tactile defensiveness." Tactile defensiveness is extreme sensitivity to different textures or touch.

In a small pilot study conducted in Cornwall, England by psychiatrists Stephen Brown and Rohit Shankar and occupational therapist Kathryn Smith, 100% of the study participants diagnosed with BPD also displayed sensory defensiveness. The authors proposed that sensory defensiveness was the true force behind the BPD symptoms.[75]

Sharon Heller, PhD quotes this study in her new book, *The Anxiety Myth*. In this book, she also states that, ""Others become defensive following any trauma that disrupts the nervous system, and especially if the trauma is severe or long-standing. Under extremely stressful conditions, an excess of the neurotransmitter glutamate kills cells, which lessens the brain's ability to inhibit sensory input and resets the sensory threshold." [76]

When BPD is due to trauma, it is only logical that sensory defensiveness could result. However, most of the time, sensory defensiveness is related to an inborn (and probably inherited) propensity. I believe it is also very possible to be born sensory defensive and for sensory defensiveness to escalate following a trauma. I believe this is what occurred in my personal development.

Karen M Moore, MT, OTR/L also conducted a small-scale pilot study employing the "Wilbarger Brushing Protocol" with BPD sufferers.[77] The Wilbarger Brushing Protocol consists of systematic brushing of various parts of the body, using a surgical brush, which "wakes up" the nerve endings. The brushing is always followed by deep joint compression to "re-organize" the nervous system. At first, the protocol involves brushing every two hours for two weeks. After this time, brushing is performed as maintenance on an "as needed" basis.

Moore found that those who followed through with this intensive method were free of self-injury 18 months later. She proposes that often self-injury is used to help regulate a nervous system that is out of balance. I agree. Although I have not self-injured in almost a decade now, I do believe a primary reason for it was sensory regulation.

We receive data from our senses that is then processed through our brain. The brain translates this data into emotions. Therefore, emotional modulation techniques such as those taught in DBT are helpful, but sensory modulation techniques affect the nervous system far more deeply, and in many cases, permanently. Sensory modulation is a necessary foundation for emotional modulation to be effective.

I've also used Listening Therapy since May of 2006. Listening Therapy is a powerful technique that actually may improve concentration, attention, balance and coordination over time. All of these techniques regulate and balance the nervous system. Since I have used them, I have experienced a deeper sense of internal organization and overall calming.

Since these techniques may only be offered by a licensed occupational therapist, a doctor's order is required, in order to receive services. Without a diagnosis of autism, ADD or SID, it may be difficult to convince your doctor of the need. However, if you explain how studies done have showed some effectiveness of OT techniques with BPD, this may encourage your doctor to allow you to experience it.

Another essential tool that I use is a "sensory soothing kit." I have a small bag that I carry in my purse. It contains: ear plugs, aromatherapy oils to inhale when I'm feeling stressed, scented lip gloss, hand lotion, facial tissues, a few hard candies, chewing gum, my "take as needed" medication and emergency phone numbers to call for support as needed. The contents of your kit may vary. However, carrying the kit provides a sense of security, although I rarely need to use it anymore.

Occupational Therapists have also found that some of the same tools that soothe autistic adults (and other people who have SID) also work to soothe BPD sufferers: examples include, weighted blankets (particularly fleece) or weighted vests, wrist or ankle pads or lap pads. I use all of these at different times, and I also use therapeutic cushions to sit on at times.

I was also placed on an "intensive sensory intervention plan," which is a highly structured sensory diet program. "Sensory diet" refers to the sensory activities you choose to use when you are feeling out of sync emotionally or in response to sensory reactions to your environment.

Some Examples:

Proprioceptive/Oral/
Under-Stimulated or Unfocused: chewing gum, carrot sticks, apple munching, vegetable chips
Oral/Over-Stimulated: drinking any beverage through a straw, especially a milkshake (very calming)

Whole Body: I have an exercise ball and I roll on it. I lie on it and roll on my back or my stomach. I can really feel my body! The highest point of awareness is when I am rolling and the ball stops. Do you remember as a child, the feeling you had when you landed from the slide on the playground? That feeling is similar. When I am out of touch with my body, I roll. I also laugh and feel calmer when I'm through!

Vestibular:
Since May 2005, I have owned a "vestibular disc" and I have been doing exercises on it that were recommended by my occupational therapist. She recommends these exercises to improve my balance. I also work on the exercise ball to achieve the same effects. Swinging on a swing-set or jumping on a trampoline help both aspects of the core nervous system (the vestibular AND the proprioceptive!)

The Wilbarger Protocol is the best method for decreasing "tactile defensiveness." However, I have learned to surround my environment with soft, cuddly things, such as fleece, velvet and pure cotton. My bed is covered in silky and fleecy blankets, throws and pillows. I also keep a collection of scented soaps, shampoos and body lotions. Of this collection, some are "soothers" and others are "stimulators." I have learned to use the appropriate ones during times that I need sensory or emotional "balancing."

Step Five
How To Make Choices
By Learning Emotional Modulation Skills

The most important part of the emotional healing process is the first step, to create an environment for healing and for the recovery of integrity to begin. Your "inner child" may have been wounded, and you may experience this as "screaming out to be heard." This is an opportunity for you to witness to and comfort this aspect of yourself in her pain.

In order to take care of your inner child, you create within yourself an accepting observer to be present to him or her. This observer is completely non-judgmental and accepting of all of the feelings, thoughts and experiences of the inner child. This way, when the feelings start to come out, you are never completely identified with them, because part of you is always detached and observing them.

How much should you detach? Only enough so that you can effectively offer your inner child a witnessing presence. If you detach too much, you may be unable to express your feelings in their entirety. If you detach too little, you may panic, feeling overwhelmed with the feelings. This is why creating a witness to your pain is a technique which takes practice for many people. Through practice, you will be able to create an environment in which you are your own perfect parent, loving and accepting the child until all of the pain has been expressed to resolution.

There are several helpful techniques in creating the observer to be present for the child. The first technique is learning to be aware of your breath. Your breath provides cleansing and healing for body and soul. It is helpful to spend a few days just becoming aware of your breathing during the day. You could carry a reminder, such as wearing a bracelet or carrying a timer, to direct you back to your breath, throughout the day.

Another component of creating a compassionate observer is to meditate on "love." Try to picture what love means to you. Call up all the feelings and memories you have associated with love, or just repeat the word "love" to yourself many times over. Meditating on love will help remind you to witness to your feelings impartially and to accept yourself without judgment.

As your memories, wounds and pain begin to arise, allow them to pass straight through you. Know that as you accept them without judgment, they are released. Feel the feelings fully and use the power of your breath to push them through. Use meditating on love to remind yourself that you are perfect just the way you are, that there is nothing to judge or condemn. Accept and love all that you are and have been.

As you are moving through this process, it may be useful to do certain things to create an effective external healing environment. Set aside a place in your home for healing, such as your bed or sofa. Set up this area with all your creature comforts, such as blankets, soft toys, tissues, a cup of tea, and whatever you desire to help you to feel nurtured through this process. Consider creating a "sensory room," using suggestions from the previous step, in order to enhance effectiveness.

Also, as you are becoming the observer and witnessing to your pain, you may consider crossing your arms over your chest in order to "hold" yourself. I found this technique to be very powerful in encouraging healing to move through me. Another thing that helped me at certain times was to carry a "power object" such as a crystal, to remind me to stay in the observer role. Holding it while reliving or re-experiencing feelings is a helpful focusing tool for maintaining the observer role.

Some people become needy and believe that only others can meet those needs. People believe that they need others in order to be happy, and so when those others are gone, they suffer. They may relive the trauma of their original abandonment when the one they love goes away.

People are not really healing during these episodes, because they are simply re-enforcing the messages of the original trauma. They are telling themselves they cannot heal, that they cannot take care of themselves. They sit and cry and suffer, feeling victimized because the one they love has gone away. How dare he do this to me! There is no comfort, only tears and rage.

People re-experiencing abandonment wounds often "act out" from rage and pain by hurting themselves or placing themselves in dangerous situations. These people have a difficult time when their therapists go away on a vacation.

The therapists usually make sure that someone else is able to be available to offer them extra support during the time of crisis. The patients are sometimes given "transitional objects" to help remind them of the therapist's presence when he is gone. They are told to practice coping skills to get them through the crisis, but there is no emphasis traditionally put on changing the messages of the original trauma in order to restore wholeness to the psyche.

In order to heal from these wounds, make sure to reassure yourself that you are not in the middle of a terrible tragedy. You are in the midst of a powerful and unique healing opportunity. During this powerful time, you have the chance to transform your life forever. Take advantage of this. Listen to all of the stories you have been telling yourself about how you are a victim, that others don't care if they hurt you, that you need them to be whole.

Don't judge yourself for having these thoughts, just listen. Now, tell yourself the truth. You are a strong and capable person. Breathe this truth deeply inside of you. You can love yourself through this. Learning to love yourself is like building up a muscle. At first, your ability will feel weak, but the more you practice, the stronger you will become.

Summary of Emotional Healing Techniques

You feel a deep, crushing pain inside. It feels so excruciating you wonder if you will survive the pain. You may begin to contemplate suicide as a comfort to yourself because you are desperate for a relief from the pain. You may begin to beat yourself up emotionally because you blame yourself. If you suffer from post-traumatic stress disorder or borderline personality disorder, perhaps you begin to scratch your skin deeply, or reach for a knife.

At the center of your soul, there is a huge, gaping hole. It is a deep wound from a traumatic injury that may have occurred within your first four years of life. It wasn't okay for you to need comfort or love. It wasn't okay for you to express feelings or to have needs or desires.

Maybe instead of of being held and cuddled, you were physically, emotionally or sexually abused. The center of your soul was crushed. It doesn't matter if you are twenty, thirty, forty or fifty years old now. You still hurt. You still need to heal. The good news is, you can heal through becoming your own perfect parent. All it takes is love, compassion and commitment. Here is how to begin the process:

View your pain and your wounds with compassion.   Do not judge your feelings, wounds and reactions. Fill your mind and heart with compassion and direct it towards yourself.

Practice holding yourself. Try crossing your arms over your chest when you are hurting. Breathe in deep. Rock if you need to. Wrap yourself up in a blanket. Imagine that you are holding a precious baby and that baby is yourself.

Do not avoid the feeling. Just sit with it and hold it, as you would a crying baby. Breathe deeply and accept your pain compassionately.

When you are experiencing pain, make sure the adult part of you is present so that you can witness the child's pain. This assures that you will not get overwhelmed with the feelings. Leave yourself notes around the house to remind you to "find the adult you" in a crisis.

Allow the "child you" to write to the "adult you." Sometimes, writing with the non-dominant hand can help this process along. Your goal is to listen to your feelings and honor and accept them with love and compassion.

Meditate on love. Imagine how love feels. Try to remember any of the times you have felt loved. In cases of severe trauma, as in post traumatic stress disorder or borderline personality disorder, this may be difficult. Call up memories of feeling happy, bonded or at peace, or try to imagine what this would feel like.

Pray to God for healing and believe that your prayer will be heard. If you have difficulty with the idea of God, try praying to the "Great Spirit" or "Spirit of Love." Praying continuously for healing can accomplish powerful results.

Let the feelings move through you with ease as you breathe deeply and release them. Love yourself, accept your feelings, and then release the pain. Don't worry about analyzing your experiences or thoughts. Just let it all go. Understanding your pain won't help you to heal, only accepting it and releasing it will.

Don't give up no matter what. Be patient with yourself and be committed to love yourself no matter what! You are worth it!

Step Six
Defining Yourself
By Finding the "Blessing" in the "Curse"

US

As we sleep our feet are locked.
Our legs are bent up to our chest.
You are older than I
but we are in utero together,
for an instant
born at the same time.
Sharing a womb,
becoming our mother,
we feed like a fetus on the food of night.
We are merged in the primeval origins of us.

In the story of Mary Poppins by P.L. Travers,[78] there is a touching scene in which the reader is allowed to overhear a conversation between two babies in a crib. The babies, John and Barbara, are highly articulate and insightful. They are wondering about how it is that the adults in their environment do not have certain abilities to sense the environment of the world around themselves.

Mary Poppins informed them that adults were all once capable of the sensory abilities of babies, to understand "the starling and the wind and what the trees say and the language of the sunlight and the stars." The children struggled to understand how it could be that the adults forgot, and when they had grasped this, they burst into pitiful tears for the loss the adults had undergone of such a close relationship with nature and the world.

Freud referred to the use of "primitive intuition" and the resultant "poetic feeling of oneness" with everything as the "oceanic state." The "oceanic state" is similar to the experience of the "Poppins babies" in the story. Although we know that babies are not capable of having such sophisticated conversations, P.L. Travers causes us to wonder what they would say if they could talk articulately.

Life in this infantile "oceanic state" has no boundaries between people or with things, such as wind and birds and even the blanket on which they nap. The infant truly has no sense of separateness. He or she is, in fact, one with everything, and has no sense, whatsoever, of a separate identity.

What does this have to do with living in a the psychological state most associated with "BPD?" Some people diagnosed with BPD (and some people diagnosed with autism spectrum disorders) remain in this state all the time. Donna Williams is a graduate, lecturer and researcher who was diagnosed with severe autism as a child.

She describes her experience this way:

> Until I was eight, I was like a sleepwalker. I had no sense of myself - where I stopped and physical objects began. It was as if I merged with everything and had no boundaries - the most extraordinary sensation, like being permanently on drugs. I had no sense of time - I could watch the clouds for hours.[79]

Not only do I remember this, but quite a bit of her description is still true for me. For instance, I still have almost no conception of time. Often, I have difficulty structuring my time, and I often will get so lost in an experience that hours pass and I forget to do other things. The awareness I have gained of my body has been through occupational therapy as an adult. I still feel like a "sleepwalker" at times, in the sense that Donna describes.

However, I have learned quite a lot about "boundaries" through the years. I did eventually gain the awareness of "where I stop and the rest of life starts," although sometimes I choose not to remember that. Some days, I still just want to sit and watch the clouds, experiencing myself as part of the sky.

For the more severe forms of autism or BPD that improve over time, or for a few more mildly impaired patients, there are merely moments in which people experience return to this "infantile" state of mind.

There are those moments when a patient will become attached to a therapist and see the therapist as only an extension of herself. He is not a person in his own right. He is only a being who responds to her needs, and she does not want the therapist to have a life outside of being with her. The same scenario may be true in a romantic relationship.

Alternately, the patient continually yearns for that "mystical" or "oceanic feeling." She tries to get it through drugs, alcohol or total merger with another person or experience. Or, the patient will act on whims or passing fancies, on impulse based on just a "feeling." Sometimes, she does not know who she is, where she starts or stops or where others begin. Helping other people is often only a way for her to help herself.

Although I could give a multitude of other examples, it is enough to say that the hypnotic "spell" that lingers over the infant is ever-present with many adults with various psychological or neurological diagnoses. Something different happened in early development, and the "hypnotic spell" never completely broke. The babies in the Mary Poppins story swore adamantly that they would not forget, even though Mary Poppins assured them that they would.

People diagnosed with BPD, (as well as those diagnosed with autism spectrum disorders) often do not forget. This is every bit as much a curse as it is a blessing. As a result, they are prone to very frightening experiences, since other people they find in the world have "forgotten." These "other people in the world" are not motivated in adulthood by infantile needs, but people diagnosed with BPD are.

Since I believe every hardship has a hidden blessing somewhere inside of it, I will say that people diagnosed with BPD are more aware of their connectedness to nature, feeling intensely connected with the environment, including the effects of subtle changes in weather. People diagnosed with BPD (as well as members of the autistic spectrum) are often more sensitive to children and animals, understanding their experience and naturally finding grounds to identify with them.

Often, it has been said that borderline parents may help to create borderline children. In a certain sense, this has to be the case. People diagnosed with BPD have not reached some of the same developmental milestones that are required in order to help children to reach goals such as those of identity and separateness. They tend to be self-absorbed much of the time, and may have difficulty relating to the needs of others. Yet, positively, they do have a certain sense of "real empathy" that has been neglected to have been seen by most professionals.

As mentioned above, this empathy often shows as understanding in a natural and genuine way how small children or animals may be feeling. It is so easy for the clinical eye to see psychopathology, without noticing the hidden blessings the same disorders may bring.

I was surprised to learn that people diagnosed with Asperger's Syndrome are also considered not to have empathy. This is also "not exactly true." It's situational. For instance, If I walk into a room and someone is crying or stomping around throwing things in anger, but I am deep in thought OR entranced by something interesting I'm looking at out the window, I will appear to the other person to be the most cold hearted person in the world.

Get my attention. Tell me what you're feeling. I will absolutely care and listen to you and support you.

My mother used to call me "Mrs. Spock." One day, she was crying about a beautiful tree that had been cut down and suddenly, she snapped at me, "You have no feelings. I could not have given birth to such an unfeeling daughter."

"If I have no feelings, then why did that hurt?" I asked, logically.

I have very deep feelings. They are even more intense than some that others have. I also have empathy for situations other people will never be able to comprehend. I have natural sensitivity for those on the autistic spectrum and also those who have experienced trauma.

Everyone, besides me, with autism or not, has the most empathy for what they have personally experienced. If their experiences are outside the norm a lot, well, that's what they have empathy for.

It used to be that "imagination" was considered not to exist for those of us with autism. Well, that's obviously NOT true. We're some of the most creative people alive. But, ask me to imagine my life 1,5 or 10 years from now OR ask me to imagine what goes on in someone else's head and I will have quite a lot of difficulty. That doesn't mean that I don't care and don't want to learn.

Mourning

It has been said that people who have borderline personality disorder (and also many diagnosed with autism) are not capable of going through the normal mourning or grieving process. Yet, there are many things that they genuinely grieve for that the general population does not: going through life feeling incomplete, being deprived of "normal" experience, not having bonded with a parent the way that "whole" individuals have, and the endless search for filling the void that a lack of bonding has created itself.

In the case of those diagnosed with "borderline personality disorder," later in life, after years of hospitalizations, failed relationships and career setbacks, a mourning for what could have been if she had only been more "healthy" often occurs. These are genuine grounds for deep and painful grief that non-people diagnosed with BPD never have to experience.

In the illustration above, however, the babies, John and Barbara, cried piteously for the fact that they would soon have to give up their "oceanic" infantile experience. This is an event, which could never be anticipated by an infant, but, as P.L. Travers has illustrated, the experience would be quite traumatic if an infant could anticipate it. In the case of the borderline personality, however, we have a situation in which someone having the adult mind the babies in the story were attributed to have possessed can actually see the future and anticipate such loss, and must go through a similar experience on a very real level.

There are so many things to give up, such as mourning for:

- what childhood could have been
- what adult life could have been
- childish ways and habits that have been a source of comfort throughout adulthood (including those that are self-destructive and maladaptive)
- hope that anything outside of yourself can make you whole
- realizing you do not have the resources within yourself to become "whole" at this point in time

- constantly having to confront an imperfect world with its incompetence and shortcomings to fulfill your overwhelming needs.

Most people not diagnosed with BPD or autism have accomplished these tasks so long ago that they can scarcely remember them. But for the person diagnosed with BPD or autism, it is a matter of survival to hold on to some of these mechanisms, because other coping skills are not as strong as they could be. Not operating from the standpoint of a whole and separate self often permeates every second of every day, whether they are sixteen or sixty-five.

Many times those labeled with these diagnoses seek out caregivers, either through lovers or through their support network. Often, they are seeking ardently to find someone to provide what their parents did not. It is even possible to begin to have delusions that these others are actually their parents. A common example is the delusion that their therapist is actually their parent. This is because they wish so desperately at times that this were true.

These needs that you long for can be met in adult ways as you learn to care for yourself with the assistance of your therapist. In many ways, your therapist may play a parental role and help you to develop in ways that you did not as a child, but your therapist can never be your parent. No one else can actually be your parent but your parents, and the time for them to help you is over. It is too late for them to give you what you needed then.

Thus, in order to become empowered to develop the immature parts of yourself, from an adult vantage point, you will need to accept and mourn that you did not get what you needed once. The good news is that it is possible, through conscious effort, to become your own perfect parent. Even if your best efforts fail, you are capable of reassuring yourself that you are an adult who can take care of yourself. Sometimes, such a simple reminder can shut down the sense of feeling like a helpless child.

EXPANDED APPLICATIONS
For those with BPD or on the Autistic Spectrum/ related disorders, such as NLD, ADD, and SID:

The grief process described above is probably also a description you can relate to. Any of these different types of neurological functioning may lead you to feel unbalanced, as if parts of you are very young and parts of you are older than you seem. Living with neurological differences that create uneven development of skills is often immensely frustrating for people who are absolutely trying their best. In addition, for the most part, these are "invisible disabilities," so people hold the expectation that you are going to be able to perform in areas that you can't.

This does not mean that you have a "child part" and an "adult part," or a "retarded part," and a "brilliant part." This is a concept that took me a very long time actually to integrate, but it's true. You are a uniquely designed individual, an adult, even when you feel weak or regressed.

Reaching a stage when you are able to "let go" of the image of how you "should be," may be very painful. However, if you are experiencing a lack of balance inside, it is also important for you to remember that whether or not it resulted from genes or trauma, your life is what it is. It may be therapeutic to write out "fantasies" of what you believed you should be like or have accomplished, and then allow yourself to grieve them.

Step Seven
How Learning Boundaries Defines Who YOU Are

More importantly, with the "letting go" that so often occurs in the healing process for people with borderline personality, there is also the learning of boundaries. To picture the most extreme example of a person who has no boundaries, imagine a man or woman who walks into a neighbor's house uninvited and without knocking, who takes whatever he or she wants, and then walks back out, satisfied that the object belongs rightfully in his hands because he found it.

Imagine one year olds at a day-school taking one another's toys and clothes that are left lying around. There is not yet a concept of "mine" and "yours." Another example might be of what looks like the opposite scenario, but it actually is not. Imagine someone who allows others to come into her house uninvited and without knocking to take whatever they please. He or she will allow them to touch her in any way they please, make any sexual advances, or assault her body freely. She, as well, does not have a sense of personal boundaries. In the first scenario, our subject did not see any boundary lines, and in the second scenario, the subject could not set limits for him or herself on a physical level.

Emotional boundaries are similar. Someone with poor emotional boundaries either assumes others feel the same way she does or she assumes she feels the way others do. Feelings are contagious, like crying at a funeral when you didn't even know who died. Just because everyone else is so sad it makes you sad. When people don't know how they feel, they look around sometimes for signals of what they should feel, imitating the behaviors of those around them.

Mental boundaries are unclear and fuzzy when the borderline agrees with whoever happens to be around, and she has few opinions or viewpoints that are truly her own. Opinions are often formed based on whatever context exists. Someone can hear and understand both sides of an issue and have no ability to take a position that does not waver. Or, she will be impressionable, and believe whatever she is told by anyone she happens to respect at the time, without thinking critically.

EXPANDED APPLICATIONS

Although people diagnosed with BPD are the "most known" clinically as having "boundary issues," persons diagnosed with Asperger's Syndrome, Non-Verbal Learning Disability, Sensory Integration Disorder and Attention Deficit Disorder also have significant problems sorting through how to apply the concept of "boundaries" between themselves and other people. Social skills training is the best way to learn skills in reciprocity (the give and take) of communication, sharing of property, and living in harmony with others.

The Role of Trauma

Each individual has a certain threshold through which he or she is most comfortable and least threatened. For those who suffer from sensory integration disorder, often both sensory and emotional experiences are magnified and sometimes exponentialized. Therefore, what is an ordinary day to one person may be quite traumatic to another. Some of the most famous research about the biology of PTSD with BPD was conducted by Dr. Rinne and his associates:

Rinne and co-workers noted a hyper-responsiveness of the hypothalamic-pituitary-adrenal (HPA) axis in patients with borderline personality disorder and a history of sustained childhood abuse, lending support to the hypothesis of a relation between early traumatisation and increased HPA axis function in adulthood.[80]

Later, the article states:

However, whether the observed neurobiological dysfunctions are pre-existing—ie, due to genetic, pre-postnatal factors, or adverse events during childhood—or the consequence of the disorder itself, is unknown.

One might assume that everyone who survives profound trauma must develop long term post-traumatic stress disorder. However, this myth does not turn out to be bourne out by research. I was surprised to discover a strong genetic component to chronic or "complex" post-traumatic stress disorder (PTSD.)

Some of the early evidence for genetic influences on PTSD came from studies demonstrating that genetically distinct mouse strains reared in identical environments show variation in response to fear conditioning[81] (one of the primary neurobiological models for the etiology of PTSD.) In fact, studies have consistently found an inherited proclivity to PTSD in adulthood, based on twin studies.[82] [83] [84] Even gene studies show an emergent profile.[85] [86]

Also, an article published in the Psychiatric Times showed that parents who experienced trauma passed on PTSD symptoms to their children who had not been exposed to trauma.[87]

Over 50% of U.S. women and 60% of men report having experienced a traumatic event at some point in their lives. However, only a minority (approximately 10% of women and 5% of men) report having ever developed posttraumatic stress disorder, the most prominent psychiatric disorder associated with traumatic events.[88]

Most people experience what clinicians call an "acute stress reaction," following a severely stressful event, such as going to war, losing a family member to 9-11 or growing up with an incident of physical or sexual abuse, 20% or less who have had such experience will still suffer from reliving the trauma in the form of PTSD years later.

I wonder why some people replay traumatic scenes over and over in the form of flashbacks and nightmares, while others don't? Isn't this a type of "thought looping?" In my case, I believe it has been. I cannot even watch horror movies, because I will "thought loop" the scary scenes for up to a month after seeing the movie. If you have suffered a traumatic experience which still haunts you and causes considerable suffering on a daily basis, please remember that this is definitely not a sign of weakness on your part. You are simply biologically disposed to experience greater stress, and then to replay that stress more often later on.

One treatment that has shown promise is EMDR (eye movement desensitivization and restructuring.) I went through this treatment and it was very helpful for me. Although trauma was not the primary reason why I fit the criteria for BPD during the years I did, I did have auxillary issues with trauma which EMDR therapy helped to correct.

As I mentioned earlier in the introduction, many individuals feel they must sacrifice ever finding intimacy in relationships in order to maintain relative stability in life. This is a most disturbing trend. Judith Lewis Herman, M.D., writes about what she considers to be the "dialectic of trauma." The "dialectic of trauma" evidences itself often in contradictory attitudes and actions toward relationships. She writes,

> "Trauma impels people both to withdraw from close relationships, and to seek them desperately. The profound disruption in basic trust, the common feelings of shame, guilt, and inferiority, and the need to avoid reminders of the trauma may be found in social life, all foster withdrawal from close relationships. But the terror of the traumatic event intensifies the need for protective attachments. The traumatized person therefore frequently alternates between isolation and anxious clinging to others. The dialectic of trauma operates not only in the survivor's inner life, but also in her close relationships. It results in the formation of intense, unstable relationships that fluctuate between extremes" [89]

Not all people diagnosed with BPD endured traumatic abuse. Regardless, this very formation of intense, unstable relationships is one of the basic diagnostic criteria of borderline personality disorder. The position described above is one of very fragile boundaries. The traumatized person either needs others desperately or she desperately feels she must avoid all people to avoid further trauma. She may live out these contradictions in relationships, confusing others and ultimately driving them away.

These same dynamics are also seen in attachment disorders. Trauma does not need to be present to create attachment disorders. For example, many people on the autistic spectrum or with NLD and SID have trouble bonding due to perceptual difficulties that lead to grasping a concept of "mother" as related to "self." Difficulty with the bonding parents with caregivers, stemming form neurological differences, may create the same dynamic. Therefore, it isn't just a "dialectic of trauma," but a "dialectic of impaired relationship development."

Since you are on our way toward recovery and toward healthier relationships, it is important to be able to recognize how you have lived out these extremes in your own life. Next, it is important to realize when you feel drawn toward repeating these patterns in the present moment. It is important to accept your feelings of abandonment without trying frantically to encourage someone else to stay by your side when you are feeling clingy.

You will need to deal with low self esteem and also accept your feelings of anxiety and fear, although they can even verge on paranoia. Not being able to cope with those feelings may have led to isolation or may have caused you to throw yourself desperately into relationships. You will need to stay acutely aware in order to create this balance and moderation in your personal relationships.

You cannot deal with these feelings effectively enough to create this balance by acting on your feelings as soon as they arise. This is why I focus so much on emotional regulation and expression, which offers a positive channel for these emotions so that they will not adversely affect your relationships. The heart of emotional regulation is acceptance, or just allowing yourself to sit with the feeling and contain it.

If you are still seeking pure excitement and you are enjoying the wild "ups and downs" of relationships driven totally by your impulses and passions of the moment, a consequence to this is that you will continue to have intense, unstable relationships. You will not find "true love," or intimacy, or anything remotely approximating your romantic dreams. You will be let down. You will feel abandoned.

You will act out by threatening to hurt your lover or yourself. You need to accept that you made the decision to arrive at this outcome. It was not your lover's fault for letting you down. You have arrived at this miserable outcome because of your own choices. Because you have not thought through the consequences of your actions, you found that you paid dearly by deep disappointment, deep feelings of abandonment, and another relationship that just didn't work out. The older you get, the more frustrating it will all become.

What other choice does a love-seeking "borderline" have? One possibly unexplored choice is to work on learning balance and moderation BEFORE getting involved in a romantic relationship. If you develop balance and moderation within yourself, you will choose relationships that reflect your contented state of mind. You can do this effectively by working on the issues that you have in *The Borderline and Beyond Workbook*, in therapy, or in your support group.

Key steps I have mentioned have been:
1. **AWARENESS** of feeling as if you are moving to extremes.
2. Making a conscious **DECISION** to accept your emotions rather than react when provoked. (We react because we find our emotions unacceptable and want to fix them.)
3. Using appropriate **COPING SKILLS**.
4. Most important, **STAYING COMMITTED** to your goal of working toward healthy relationships by not letting yourself be

swayed by the temptation to become involved in relationships before you are ready.

When will I be ready for a relationship?

You are ready for a relationship when you are able to set your own mental, emotional, physical and sexual boundaries BEFORE a date or get-together, and you CONSISTENTLY follow the boundaries you have set beforehand. You are ready for a relationship when you are comfortable with being alone, but you are not "hiding out" or isolating from others. You are ready for a relationship when you call other people for support when you need it, but you don't expect them to rescue you.

Your relationships with people in general are "give and take." Your community is no longer merely your rescue team. You are an active member of your community of support and are able to offer support to others and reciprocate the help that they give to you. You are ready for a relationship when you are self-reliant, but interdependent with others. You are not feeling clingy towards your therapist. Your emotions have been stable and calm for a good length of time.

You realize that intimacy is a choice and not a need. If you are currently married or involved in a relationship and you have just read the list above, you may be asking yourself, "What about those of us who are not ready for a relationship, who just happen to be in one?" You will have a more difficult struggle. Your task is to define and exercise your own boundaries, and to follow the above-stated steps.

This may be more difficult because in many cases the relationship you are in presently has been following an altogether different set of rules for some time. Change is threatening to both parties in the relationship, and it is much easier to slip into old ways of behaving, because they are more familiar to the relationship. Change is possible, however, and you can do it if you remain COMMITTED.

The easiest way to change is to focus on accepting yourself as you are. The more you love and accept yourself, the more energized you will become to reach your goals, naturally.

Step Eight
Defining Self Through Practicing Acceptance

Acceptance is the art of letting people, situations and objects all just be themselves, without judgment. "Acceptance" is the closest I am able to come to describing pure love. Acceptance is the art of just letting things be.

For most of us, our first and only chance to experience acceptance of ourselves, just for being who we are, is during infancy. After we are born, our mothers offer us our first experience of love from outside ourselves.

When we do not fully experience ourselves as being loved unconditionally, deep "holes" within our self image emerge. Learning to love ourselves unconditionally with acceptance is the process of becoming our own mother.

Developing skill in self mothering not only facilitates emotional healing, but also forms a foundation for spiritual growth. The more secure we are within our being, the greater is our freedom to make choices in life which are positive and nurturing towards ourselves and others.

As I mentioned earlier, during infancy, we exist in a state of "oneness." In the Mary Poppins story, two babies are in a crib, crying pitifully because they have been told that they will lose their connection to "nature, what the wind is saying, the universe." As infants, we live in what Freud called the "oceanic state." We live in a state in which we feel one with a huge ocean.

According to Margaret Mahler, a neo-Freudian child development researcher, a baby does not feel small, because she does not realize that she is separate from the rest of the world. All people and things are perceived as part of the baby. It is not until later that the infant realizes she is separate from the mother, the blanket, and the world. Both the way the parents treat the baby and the natural developmental process affect the baby's experience of boundaries.

Belief in separateness and individual identity is indeed an important developmental step that all emotionally healthy people must go through. Earlier, I wrote that those diagnosed with borderline personality disorder have not completed this step of separation fully. Yet, rather than seeking to separate the rest of the way, they yearn for and seek to return to the oceanic state. Return to this state is sought through escape into the blurred boundaries of relationships or through drug or alcohol use for example.

On a deeper level, some philosophers might really say that we are all "one." All people are united in God. Although I may choose to create a separate image of who I am in the world, and define my boundaries about who can enter into my physical, emotional and mental world, I am not identified by my boundaries.

Although we are all one with God, we are still operating through separate minds. This is why it is essential to take responsibility for our own lives. It is through taking this responsibility that we are able to set up our boundaries in the external physical world. Through taking responsibility only for ourselves and not others, we learn to respect the right of everyone to "dream their own dreams," and live their own lives, judgment-free.

People diagnosed with personality disorders provide extreme examples of people not taking responsibility for themselves and of not allowing others the right to be themselves. Personality disorders (as well as autistic spectrum disorders) are often marked commonly by lack of sensitivity to the boundaries of others.

Both of these personality disorders have extremely damaged self images and poor relationships with others. Both often live their lives seeking to satisfy unmet needs from childhood. They approach others as objects who must provide for them rather than as humans. As a result of this, these people appear very needy, demanding and disrespectful of boundaries and limits.

Heinz Kohut, M.D., founder of Self Psychology, (a form of treatment used for personality disorders,) outlined two stages in development which are helpful in the therapeutic treatment of borderline and narcissistic personality disorders. I believe that Kohut's suggestions can be helpful to all of us.

Kohut's stages are called "mirroring" and "idealizing." The mirroring stage corresponds to infancy. During the "mirroring" stage, the mother is the mirror for the infant. If she smiles and coos and expresses approval for the baby's being, the baby grows up secure. If the baby is treated cruelly, casually responded to, or ignored, the baby may not sense his innate worthiness of love because the mirror does not reflect love to the baby.

If our mother reflects back our perfection, we grow up more secure in the truth of who we are. Therefore, to meditate on our own perfection is to provide our own "mirroring experience" for ourselves. Regardless of how we were raised, we can take responsibility as adults for becoming our own perfect mother.

Here is a powerful way of loving your inner baby: Just sit, breathing deeply and focusing on loving yourself in the moment, wordlessly, as though you are a perfect and wonderful infant. This is similar to what a therapist does in Self Psychology therapy. In order to help a client who did not get his needs met during the mirroring stage, a therapist creates a "mirror transference" by consistently reflecting back to the client a positive reflection of his being.

The therapist creates this mirror through words, but he also relies strongly on non-verbal methods. In many cases, self psychologists are trained to just sit without speaking with a client for hours, to give them the sense of acceptance of their being. The rationale is that the more the therapist creates the mirror transference, the more the client begins to internalize the experience of being "mirrored."

The result of facilitating a positive "mirror transference" is healthy self esteem and a strong sense of inner contentment. Although working with a therapist trained in these techniques may be helpful, it may not be necessary for everyone to work with a therapist. The most critical part of recovery is to work on mirroring alone, through meditation practices in order to assure internalization.

I discovered in my own healing work that allowing nature to reflect my being was the perfect chance for me to have the mirroring experience. I began to sense the oneness once again between myself and nature, and to merge with the peacefulness and beauty.

The second stage of development Kohut writes about is "idealizing." Idealizing is looking up to someone as being bigger and more ideal than the child is, and modeling behavior after the ideal. If the mirroring stage was successful, idealizing is simply the next step. During the pre-school years, the infant leaves the godlike sea of oneness, becomes separate and realizes she is now only a small child. To get a sense of growing bigger, the child now tries to become a "chip off the old block." As the child grows through imitation, she begins to develop a healthy sense of herself as a "doer."

A healthy sense of "doing" is built on strength in "being." When a child knows she is loved "just the way she is," her actions support and reflect her being rather than go against it. She may imitate the parents she admires, but her actions stem from her true nature.

The first stage of development is discovering "love through being" and the second type allows discovery of "love through doing." In this first "mirroring" stage, the experience of equality is important. The infant does not see the mother as bigger.

He sees her as an extension of the "oneness" he lives in. However, although she is not seen as separate, she functions as the mirror for the baby's experience of being. During the mirroring stage, a strong foundation needs to be built of "being loved just for being you." If this foundation in "being" is not strong enough, a child grows up continually trying to achieve and do things to receive approval and love. Many of these actions end up opposing the child's natural sense of integrity.

In order to build up a strong foundation within yourself of validating your "being," you can integrate mirroring techniques into your meditation practice. It is helpful to look into an actual mirror and to tell yourself you are perfectly okay, just the way you are. You could also just sit quietly, looking in the mirror for a few moments each day, just being with yourself. Notice how uncomfortable this may make you feel. Keep breathing. Sit with the discomfort. Keep looking, non-judgmentally, into your eyes.

Find a friend who is willing to practice "mirroring" with you. Sit facing each other, hold hands and look into each others eyes. Remember, you're okay just because you are, not for what you do or say or accomplish. You are perfect just because you are created in the image of God.

Fundamental, before going further, is to validate yourself profoundly just for being alive and human. When you fully accept yourself for being exactly as you are, it is easier not to reject the little things you don't like, such as your hair or your weight. However, a useful exercise is to make a list of everything "wrong" with you. Re-write the list with the truth that you are perfect just the way you are. Read the list often to validate your "being."

One of Kohut's great contributions to psychology was to introduce the concept of "deficits," as opposed to Freud's focus on "drives." Kohut refers to deficits in both mirroring and idealizing that need to be filled. When people are wounded in these areas, they are driven by trying to fill their deficits, which may be experienced as feeling like "holes" in the self.

Integral to many "mental disorders" is seeking to fill these "holes" within our souls. So many people attempt to fill deficits in mirroring with alcohol, drugs, food, sex or shopping. Not just addicts, but those suffering from depression, bipolar disorder and many impulse control disorders do this as well. Often, people try to fill idealizing wounds through the excessive drive to achieve or by devotion to a person, cause or purpose greater than themselves.

The only satisfying way to fill these holes is by our conscious choice to be responsible in this moment for loving ourselves unconditionally, and sharing that love with others. Filling these holes also starts with consciously accepting who we are, just as we are. We do not need to change anything to be worthy of love.

We can learn to validate ourselves through quieting our minds and identifying with the peaceful state of "being" that goes beyond words or labels. Through validating ourselves, we are free to make conscious choices of who we want to be. That way, we aren't driven unconsciously to achieve in order to validate our sense of being. Our "doing" becomes a natural expression of our love. Kohut's self psychological therapy is designed to help the client meet his needs for mirroring and idealizing. Through learning to internalize unconditional acceptance for both being and doing, the client feels fulfilled and is not compelled to search outside of himself to fill these deficits.

In simpler terms, the mirroring and idealizing experience provides acceptance, pure unconditional love. This love needs to be poured into the deficits (holes or wounds) in order to create a self. Through the mirroring transference, we are able to experience the oceanic state, the blessed merger with the oneness of God. Is it a return to infancy and innocence? No, it is a return to our natural state, but with the wisdom that comes from conscious return with awareness.

After we return to our natural state, we realize we are still humans who are limited. We experience feeling separate and small. Through the idealizing experience, we are able to merge with a power greater than ourselves, to belong to that which is far bigger than we are. We grow in love through both experiences.

Expanded Applications:
For those with BPD or on the Autistic Spectrum/ related disorders, such as NLD, ADD, and SID:

First of all, if you had difficulty with bonding with your mother or caregiver, or if you were unable to experience being "mirrored," it may not be anyone's fault. When an infant isn't able to take in the whole experience of a caregiver, such as being able to remember her face or scent, deficits will occur even with the best mothering. For those of us with NLD and autism, we tend to see the world in "pieces," and it may take quite a while to get a sense of the bigger picture.

Secondly, make sure that you protect yourself from abuse as an adult. I was first introduced to the concept of BPD in graduate school, when I was only 20 years old. I as fairly naïve and gullible at this time, as people who have NLD or autism spectrum disorders tend to be. I began to resonate with many of the features of this diagnosis, so I began seeing a psychologist who was a professor at that university.

He claimed he was a specialist in treating borderline personality disorder.

After nine months of therapy, he developed poor boundaries with me. He was taking me out to dinner, loaning me money and telling me things like, "I don't know how you function in life. Not only do you have BPD, but you have tons of neurological 'soft signs.'" During this time, he felt drawn to take care of me, because he viewed me as helpless and vulnerable. I moved in with him and we began a sexual relationship which chronically disturbed me. I actually lived with him for three years.

He taught me about Kohut's view of self-psychology, and his theories about how the self is developed. He tried to "heal my deficits." He was also controlling, narcissistic and critical. Although he told me I seemed to be getting increasingly clinically depressed, he refused to allow me to seek help. He was determined to be the one to "fix" me.

Eventually, when my level of inner disturbance reached unbearable proportions, I "sneaked" away to see a psychologist in Atlanta, who gradually helped me gain the courage to leave him. Because the psychologist I lived with fostered such a high level of dependency in me, whatever "borderline features" I initially had began to worsen as I came to identify more with this diagnosis and with his distorted therapeutic approach.

After leaving him, I had six psychiatric admissions within one year, which eventually culminated in a serious suicide attempt and admission to a state mental hospital. This immediately preceded my recovery process and the development of the Borderline and Beyond Self-Help Program.

I am sharing my story with you because I want to let you know the damage that inappropriate therapeutic relationships can create. If you have a neurological condition, you may have a few true "dependency needs." If you are believed to be highly intelligent, clinical professionals are likely to regard these needs as characterological, rather than real.

Because your neurological needs *are* real, it is essential that you find support for your needs that does not leave you feeling helpless, dependent and powerless. Learning to validate yourself may help you to avoid these abusive situations. Beyond doing this type of internal work is the additional step of reaching out for professional help as needed.

While practicing self-validation techniques may be tremendously helpful, especially during the "early recovery" period, eventually it is essential to reach a "bottom" level of acceptance for the reality of your life right now. If you did not have a mother, father or caregiver who was able to meet your emotional needs, you will never have one. There is no mother. There is no caregiver. It does not matter, because today, you are an adult who can take care of yourself.

At the same time, you may use your therapist, doctor, case-manager, occupational therapist or an ADD coach to assist you with life prioritization, breaking tasks down into smaller steps, and sorting through complex emotional states.

My Inspiration To Be More Fully Myself

Dr. Temple Grandin, esteemed animal researcher and probably the most well known successful woman who has autism, experienced a very positive relationship with both parents. Yet during the 50's, when she grew up, virtually every problem she experienced was automatically labeled a "psychological" symptom. Even her inability to do algebra was blamed on psychological factors.

No one at that time considered that Dr. Grandin thought only in pictures as does a child, and that algebra was not something she could visualize. It also took her quite a while to receive an accurate assessment. Even then, the cultural milieu at that time period viewed her condition more under psychological, rather than neurological terms.

In Dr. Temple Grandin's first book, *Emergence-Labeled Autistic: A True Story*,[90] Dr. Grandin originally believed she had become a "recovered autistic," because she had accomplished things few autistics could do, such as graduating from college with a major in psychology. Later in life, she realized that she still remained autistic, but had merely compensated better. She still needed additional supports, such as medication treatment and the use of her "squeeze machine" which helped her gain equilibrium with sensory issues.

For a time, Dr. Grandin visited a psychiatrist once a week, when the theory in 1956 was that autism was caused by "psychic injury." She was discouraged from following her obsessions, although her fixations calmed her and reduced her hyper-aroused levels. I relate to this experience very well, and I agree that obsessions should usually not be curtailed when they are serving a positive purpose for a child or adult.

What I admire most about Temple Grandin is that qualities that were originally considered deficits and assumed to lead to a poor prognosis for her future life eventually led to great success, because her "deficits" actually *were* her strengths. Regardless of how professionals discouraged her, Dr. Grandin makes her own choices to define who she is. She pursues her own interests, regardless of how others view them.

Another thing I appreciate most about Temple Grandin is how she always seems true to her own experience. I used to think if I could see the world exactly as it is, without a "story" of how it should be, I would then become spiritually enlightened. But Temple Grandin does see the world exactly as it is, with complex and multidimensional imagery that is difficult for her to translate into words.

Still, just as I do, she needs medications and sensory aids to function in a world that perceives so differently. Clear perception, uncluttered by words, does not necessarily lead to bliss and serenity. As soon as I realized that, many of my former spiritual beliefs became shattered. I was actually relieved to see them go, and to rejoin "reality" and "the truth of humanity!"

Few examples have impacted me as much as Dr. Temple Grandin. Being neurologically atypical, regardless of whether it is classified as ADD, NLD, SID or autism, grants the bearer the unique gift of rare and original perspective.

Because Dr. Grandin could begin to trust her own perspective and follow her own instincts and pursue her interest in developing her "squeeze machine," she was able to "open her own doors" to the future of her choice. Because of this, she was able to learn to articulate the parallels between the way she views the world and how a cow would. She is now a highly successful animal researcher who has transformed at least 2/3 of the cattle industry.

I still have much to learn about the ways I perceive and process the world, but Temple Grandin's example gave me permission to realize that whatever style I have is mine. It is okay. My personal neurological style is an asset, as long as I give myself permission to trust it.

Temple Grandin and I have both been diagnosed with "high functioning autism." However, unlike Dr. Grandin, my neurological difficulties were complicated by a traumatic relationship with my mother. Whether or not this was what led to my eleven psychiatric hospitalizations and subsequent borderline personality diagnosis, I do not know. The reason why is less important than my choice of how to cope with it. What I did at that time was to write the original *Borderline and Beyond*, a book based upon the strengths within the diagnosis and how to use them to one's advantage through the recovery process.

Still, for some reason, when I became aware of my neurological differences, I underwent a period of low self esteem for quite a while. Temple Grandin helped to turn that around for me. All I know now is that I am left with the question of how to appreciate my so called "defects," and allow them the freedom to lend me strength.

Because Temple Grandin introduced new possibilities to me, I was very pleased and honored to meet with her recently and to thank her in person. She offers a wonderful presentation of how our choices, and not the opinions of others, form our sense of identity. She has said, "My identity is formed by what I do, not what I feel."

If you have been diagnosed with borderline personality disorder, OR with an autism spectrum disorder, the potential impact of her statement on your life is the same. Remembering this simple statement and repeating it to yourself when you are under stress may help you when you are feeling overwhelmed. I know that it has often helped me.

Regardless of whether or how you have been diagnosed, the most important concept to remember is this: **Your life choices determine who you are.** Although this has always been my core message, I was helped in an extraordinary way this year by my primary psychiatrist, Dr. Lynn Ikenberry, M.D., Ph.D., because he also stressed this message very much.

The message above is his basic philosophy, which I have internalized and incorporated even more into my own work. Also, using medication has changed what used to be a struggle with choices into a more natural and effortless procedure.

Step Nine
Replacing the "Victim Mentality" with a Sense of Inner Power and Direction

As I mentioned in the beginning of this book, replacing the "victim mentality" with a sense of inner power and direction is the pivotal point of change. Earlier, I also stated, "If borderline personality disorder has any true validity as a diagnostic entity, the 'strong sense that our decisions create our identity' is the most central facet to both diagnosis and treatment.

Of course, the next question to ask oneself is, "How?"

Should I Trust Myself?

"How can I possibly trust myself? Look at the past I've lived and all of the mistakes I've made. My instincts and gut feelings have all betrayed me." To answer this question, look a little closer. Did you really trust yourself or were you surrendering your ability to make decisions to someone or something else? The title of this chapter, as usual, is a multi-layered metaphor.

Pretend for a moment that you are a spy, an espionage agent for an intelligence agency. Primary issues that surround you every day are who, if anyone, around you can be trusted. You present yourself in disguise, so that no trace of your true identity can be detected.

You present a danger to those around you, who cannot trust you. Everyone, as the old saying goes, carries a "dagger" beneath his "cloak." Your object, in this scenario, is to appear to be the most trustable agent, stab those who oppose you with the dagger, and obtain the information you require. And, you must do all of this without letting the cloak of disguise down to make you vulnerable to the daggers of others.

My question is: What kind of life is this? A paranoid, dishonest sort of life I would think. The spy in the scenario above cannot trust herself or anyone else. People diagnosed with BPD are often in disguise, because, lacking a strong sense of identity, they go about impersonating others and playing roles.

Instead of seeking information as a goal, the person diagnosed with BPD seeks persons to satisfy unmet needs from childhood instead. Any one or any thing which is willing to and able to supply this for the time being is fair game. And, when these objects of satisfaction turn to disappoint the borderline, the "dagger" of borderline rage is often felt. However, being by nature irrepressibly vulnerable and without boundaries, the dagger of the other person the borderline has run to is usually deep inside the borderline's heart before the realization that the cure for the incompleteness inside is a delusion.

In other words, following this metaphor, a person who carries the borderline diagnosis is like a very bad spy. She never gets what she's gone after, and she almost always gets stabbed in the process. In order to get what she's looking for, she will need to look within herself to find out who she really is and learn to trust this person. Then, she will not need to wear the cloak of disguise which is covering nothing at all underneath. She will still need to wear the cloak of protection from the daggers which surround us all. These are also known as boundaries. I look at this as a two part process.

First, she will need to understand what draws her to dangerous people and things. She has surrendered herself to a negative power, and she has given up her ability to choose and think and be responsible for herself. Her endeavors will fail to obtain what she needs by going this route. Then, she will need to get to know herself and develop the strength within herself to resist giving in to this negative power.

In each of the following "practice steps," I explore with you how to generate a sense of inner power and direction, drawing heavily upon the use of imagination, creativity, and natural resources which most people have, who are diagnosed with BPD. Through developing a better understanding of personal strengths and resources, it becomes more natural to draw on and eventually rely on them in any time of need.

The first step in this process is "detangling" truth from negativity and illusion!

First Practice Exercise:
Bambi Must Die

When you read the title of this subsection, what emotions move through your body? Do you feel shock, anger, horror, sadness, humor, or concern for the mental health of the author? What images move through your mind? Do you begin to see the childhood movie or the story that was told to you as a child? Do you remember the feelings you had as Bambi's mother was being shot?

Do you remember the feelings of abandonment, betrayal, lack of safety, and fear that you felt? Do you remember thinking about how bad and mean the hunters were who shot Bambi's mother? Do you remember the overwhelming fear that the abandoned, unprotected Bambi must have felt? If you can hold these images and feelings solidly in your mind, you can begin to see clearly the stories of the judge and the victim:

The world is not a safe place. The world should be a safe place. It is not and because of that, life is unjust. Mean people hurt good animals, personifications of "good people." Innocence is not protected. It will be slaughtered. This is the mindset of fear.

Disney's portrayal of Bambi the baby deer has nothing to do with a real deer. A real deer is swift and strong. If its mother is shot by a hunter, the deer does not tell itself stories about abandonment and forsakenness. A real deer does not feel sorry for itself or judge those who kill. After all, we live in a predatorial universe. This is the natural way of our world at this time.

Helen Keller once said, "Security is mostly superstition. It does not exist in nature." Animals know this, instinctually. Still, rather than live life in a fear-filled, paranoid manner, animals live in peace and harmony among predators. They are alert to the possibility that death could occur at any instant, while still enjoying each moment of their lives.

Animals live in innocence, in Eden. They live in innocence even if their parents are killed by predatory animals or humans. Although they may temporarily experience grief, just as humans do, they move on with their lives a lot more easily. They are biologically predisposed to survive and to thrive in adversity.

Humans, however, are not like this. Humans are a lot more like Bambi. That is because the "Bambi story" has been created by the human mind. Such behavior is not natural and instinctual. How do humans live out the Bambi story? They believe that they are vulnerable. They believe they are victims. They believe that the world is not a safe place, and they create stories judging others for making it that way. Then, they make excuses and justifications about how fulfilling their dreams isn't possible.

How often do you find yourself in your adult life, living and acting as if you were Bambi? And when you do, what happens in those moments to your creative energy? What happens to your ability to live, laugh, love and enjoy life for it's own sake, in this moment, where life is happening?

This is why I am proposing that Bambi must die. Now, I enjoy Disney's cartoons as much as anyone. I believe that Bambi is adorable, and if she was killed on the screen, I would feel horrified and look away. But Bambi is a metaphor for feeling like a victim. More importantly, she isn't even real.

When you are feeling afraid and victimized in life, how often do you just pet your inner Bambi on the head, saying, "It's okay. I'll take care of you against the big, bad, scary world." In doing so, do you realize in those moments you are actually buying in to the "mindset of fear" by trying to control it? How much energy does it take to try to create a false sense of security with our lives? When we are truly honest, do we see that most of our energy usually go towards creating that false sense of security?

The mindset of "acceptance for what is" is natural and requires no effort, none at all. The real you is a lot like the natural deer that lives in the natural forest. Nature involves deer just being deer, hunters just being hunters, and you just being you. No judgment, no victimization, just a peaceful day in the forest. Imagine yourself full of an abundance of creative energy to express whatever you want in this moment, fear-free. Imagine a life that is not ruled by fear, with no judge and victim controlling your life. What creative power could you have if you were not held back by beliefs that are not based on natural reality? Why not let Bambi die today?

Step Ten
Practicing Belief in Yourself
While Fighting Destructive Impulses

In one version of the movie, *Peter Pan,* mermaids lift their seductive heads over the surface of the smoky, foggy waters that surround Neverland. Peter says to Wendy, "The mermaids are here to give us a message. We need to receive the message, but we need to be careful. The mermaids are seductive and if you aren't careful, they will pull you into the waters and drown you." The mermaids deliver an important message which helps the children greatly. But then, Wendy is captivated by the luring gaze of one of the mermaids. Wendy is so captivated that she loses herself and begins to sink into the waters with the mermaid. Peter pulls her back, saving her life.

Our minds are like this. Our minds create illusion that what we are seeking is "out there" rather than within ourselves. Our minds tell us stories that keep us continually caught up in chasing empty illusions. These mirages captivate us deeply within their web until we completely forget who we are. Illusions like, "If only I were with my former lover again, everything would all be well," and "If only I were someone else or could achieve my goal, I could get to a place where I can arrive at peace and happiness."

So often, we are conditioned to believe that we will be happy "tomorrow," and so we lose ourselves in trying to accomplish goal after goal, even though we are never satisfied. Many people become "possessed" by their goals and objectives.

Like Wendy, they begin to lose themselves, as they sink into a psychological "abyss." Do we need to hear the message of the mermaids? Yes, we do. Often, we could hear an important message to help us determine the direction of our lives and where we really want to put our energy. It is important to witness this message, honor it, but not to believe it or allow it to possess us.

Another parallel is within the recent *Lord of The Rings* movie. Do you remember the way the ring possessed Smeagol and threatened to overwhelm Frodo? Like the mermaids, the ring also has a seductive power. It has a hypnotic, driving pull. It craves to be owned, possessed, as though an object "out there" can make us whole.

Any time we depend on external people and organizations outside ourselves for approval, recognition, or affirmation, we allow ourselves to become possessed. The ring symbolizes the illusionary pull of our minds. When you look at your mind with awareness, from the standpoint of the observer, you become freed to recognize and resist these illusions before they pull you deep into the waters and drown you. You can seize the awareness of your authentic self and your true integrity before a seductive illusion transforms you into a demon while promising you freedom and power. Be strong. Do not allow yourself to become possessed.

The truth does not need for you to believe it. It just is. Illusions have a driving desire to possess you. They want to be pursued and believed. They long for you to invest your energy into them. Consider this to be like a scientific "formula:" The more strongly you feel pulled to believe in something, and the more you are afraid to question it, the higher is the likelihood that you are believing an illusion. The more strongly you remember what is true and who you are, the more you are freed to resist these lies and to laugh, play, create, and enjoy your life.

Once you learn to determine what is true about what you really want and which direction you choose to travel in your life, the next step is to learn to use your previously "sabotaging" tendencies in ways that are helpful to you.

Step Eleven
Look for Hidden Choices
(or Magical Thinking and
How To Use It To Your Advantage)

In L. Frank Baum's novel, *Queen Zixi of Ix or The Story of the Magic Cloak*,[91] he tells the story of a young girl whose life was filled with pain and loss and trauma. The little girl's nickname was "Fluff," and she and her brother Bud were orphans. The children were left with their Aunt Rivette, a cruel and stern woman who physically and emotionally abused the children. Fluff cried non-stop day and night.

One night, after having to sleep in a cold stable, Fluff was weeping miserably because of the huge burden of her unhappiness. A fairy named Ereol appeared and gave her a magic cloak which had been woven by fairies. He told her that while she wore the cloak, she could have one wish granted. The little girl said that all she wanted was to be happy. After putting on the coat, she felt immeasurable happiness.

Little Fluff has discovered the use of a boundary, a protective cloak, to shield her from reacting to the circumstances around her. The beauty of this story is that I believe that this cloak could have been truly endowed with magical powers, or the cloak could have been any ordinary object that little Fluff believed in. Fluff could have discovered the same result either way. That is why, in this segment, we examine more closely the power of belief.

Many people engage in magical thinking. "Magical thinking" is having the belief that a person, place, thing or idea can instantly make all of your problems go away, or make you feel happy and secure, or that "only this object" has the power to make you whole. This sensation often feels like the "I've got-to-have-its." It can make behavior seem demanding to others who will often lose patience.

Can you relate to this? Take a look at a few examples to see if any resonate with you!

Examples:
If only _____ will go out with me, everything will be wonderful.
If I have a chocolate ice-cream cone or two, I'll feel better.
If only I buy this object, I'll never want to kill myself again.
If I can cut myself just one more time, I'll get it out of my system and I might never want to do it again.

Using Magical Thinking to Your Advantage

- When your are caught up in thought patterns similar to the ones listed above, be aware that you are using magical thinking.

- Try to stop your usual use of the practice. If you continue to do what you did before, you will not get what you want and you will become more unhappy and more upset.Instead, try to use intentionally one of the techniques listed below.

New Magical Techniques:

1. Purchase one object (a rock, a necklace, a stuffed toy, etc.) or find an object at home which comforts you, such as those mentioned above, or a photograph or religious object. Choose an object that you believe can restore you to a state of calm and peace.
2. Have an alternate object in case you cannot find the first one. Go to these objects first before seeking others.

Notes: It might be better to be able to calm yourself without using a "crutch," but sometimes people need things that they can feel and hold on to "ground" themselves when they cannot find peace within themselves. I have learned since originally writing this that these objects, such as I have always used, are called "power objects" in many Native American traditions.

3. Carry your "power objects" with you in a pocket or purse.
4. Another option is to imagine you have a "**magic amulet**" to help you. Picture vividly its color, texture, and material. Call this image up when you are feeling uneasy or nervous.
5. **Imagining beautiful scenes** helps some people. Make these exercises very personal to you and you alone. You do not need to share this practice with anyone.

Notes: You can even **invent magic words or phrases** that will help you feel more secure at times when you need them. Remember, though, that as much as these things can make you feel better, stay calm, or "keep it together" for a while, they are NOT A CURE-ALL and definitely NOT A SUBSTITUTE FOR THERAPY. These are merely short-term survival measures to prevent other forms of magical thinking from taking control over your life and making you worse than before. Also, most people are able to apply them in a light-hearted way. Recovery can finally be fun!

Expanding Your Use of
the Power of Imagination & Visualization

The power of imagination cannot be underestimated in winning the fight against self-destructive impulses, intrusive thoughts, and compulsive urges. Powerlessness is usually felt strongly as the feeling of being drowned or overwhelmed by forces beyond one's control.

The force cannot be denied to be within ourselves, a part of our own mental process, but the "force" continues to be experienced as foreign, and even in some circumstances, seems to be coming from a source outside of ourselves.

This type of thinking has been something clinicians might refer to as "ideas of reference." People diagnosed with BPD often grow to live in fear of themselves. "If I'm hurt or sad I might get depressed or start crying and not be able to stop. If I get angry I might fly into an uncontrollable rage or self-mutilate. If I'm happy I might turn into a maniac and do something crazy and impulsive. If I can't stop thinking of suicide I might have to act on it so that the thoughts will go away."

In other words, your mind does not feel like your own, your emotions do not feel like your own, and your body definitely does not feel like your own. When your core problem is a lack of identity, your own experiences often feel foreign to you. Many clinicians wonder why people diagnosed with BPD can often be so seemingly convinced that they are helpless in many ways and need to depend on others emotionally.

Imagine yourself in a similar position and imagine the task of trying to convince yourself that you have the power to control your thoughts, feelings, actions, and even your destiny. You want to believe it. You really do. Believing this could solve so many of your problems and you know it. So, you decide to begin this journey. Where do you start?

Trying to think positively is a good start. Empowering affirmations, such as, "I believe I am in control," may help, but only minimally. This is because you are continually confronted with your old ways of thinking, feeling and behavior, (that "ingrained, chronic problem" that is, by definition, why the person has been diagnosed with a personality disorder to begin with!)

Many traditional approaches don't help much in handling the problem. The problem is that they are other people's ideas. Imagine how much more empowering it can be to devise personal, unique and original approaches to dealing with these "demons." Much therapeutic guidance in devising these may be needed, but the most essential ingredient is for the overwhelmed and helpless-feeling patient to begin to feel a sense of power and control over what is going on inside.

Suggestions
For People Who Have BPD or PTSD or Intrusive
Thoughts Associated with OCD

Below area few examples of some meditations and visualizations that I find successful. Use them as models to find ways to solve your own unique difficulties. If they work exactly as written, by all means continue to use them. When you are feeling out of control (regardless of the techniques you are currently using) remember to use the positive force of imagination to speed your healing.

○ When intrusive images appear in your mind (scenes of past trauma, or negative things happening in the future), imagine that you are looking at a picture instead of a "3-D" scene, and imagine that you can wash the image away with soap and water, to "purify your mind." You could also try imagining you're looking at a tape in a VCR and erase over it. Or, try changing the scene any way at all to make it different or less threatening. Be creative!

○ Picture yourself in a large cylindrical container, the size of a small room. The walls of the container are clear and strong. Nothing from the outside can come inside to hurt you. As the scenes pass by outside the room, picture yourself inside the room, safe and secure.

Look for Hidden Choices
Example Two

When I went to see the new Harry Potter film, *Harry Potter and the Chamber of Secrets,* I was drawn to a character who appears to wreck havoc in Harry's life. He is a small two foot creature called, "Dobby the House Elf." Dobby is a character that is difficult to despise or hate, because he is so touchingly vulnerable and well meaning. Yet every time we see him appearing, we have a tendency to tense up and cringe, because we know that something horrible is likely to happen.

Dobby sabotages everything Harry is trying to do in his life, yet Dobby has the "best intentions," believing he is helping Harry. Dobby's master has told him that he must prevent Harry from going back to school and from staying in touch with his friends from school. So Dobby, the house elf, steals all of the letters from Harry's friends, so that he cannot read them. When Harry and his friends try to return to school in the flying car, Dobby makes sure that they are seized by a giant tree that thrashes the car with the children inside.

Dobby's cruel master punishes him continuously. However, Dobby seems to enjoy punishing himself, proclaiming things like, "Dobby has ironed his hands." In fact, just when Harry is at his angriest is when Dobby exclaims that he has already punished himself. This encourages Harry to back down and leave him alone. Dobby doesn't like the behavior he is doing, but he feels powerless to stop it. Dobby presents some borderline behavior traits, because he is continuously self-depreciating and living his life governed by fear. Dobby does not display spontaneous borderline impulsiveness, because he never goes against his master.

However, Dobby feels powerless to stop his own behavior, which is very borderline in itself. He has no real sense of self. His behavior towards self and others is continuously destructive. Dobby is both terrified of being abandoned by his master and yearning to be free. So Dobby displays some very basic borderline personality dynamics.

In order to become free of his master, Dobby's master has to give him the gift of a piece of clothing. In other words, Dobby is totally bare, exposed. He has no protection whatsoever from the onslaughts of judgment from himself and others, and the feeling of victimization. Imagine that a borderline has a similar "internal master" pushing him to do certain things. He may not even be aware that he has internalized these "orders and directives" from the judgmental authority of other people. He has "no clothing," no defense of his own.

At the end of the movie, Harry Potter tricks Dobby's master by placing one of the master's socks in a book and asking the master to hand it to Dobby. Dobby opens the book, the sock falls out, and Dobby is free. The audience celebrates with rave applause. In this instant, Dobby has accidentally been given a method to reclaim his power and to become his own master. No more does Dobby need to do things that go against his integrity, that harm himself and others. All it took was being presented with this symbol of a piece of clothing.

I offer you this symbol, this piece of clothing: Your choices define who you are, so become more aware of what your choices are. You don't have to live your life in fear for yourself and other people. You don't have to punish yourself. You don't have to hurt yourself so that other people won't hurt you first. You don't have to hurt yourself because you are overwhelmed with emotional pain, or because you are so overcome with anguish because you are acting against your own integrity.

You don't have to live life based on fear and reacting to fear. You can be free. All it takes is to make the commitment in this moment to love yourself with all your heart, never to abandon yourself again. Extend this same commitment to yourself in every moment until it becomes a deeply engrained habit, and you will become your own master of love.

EXPANDED APPLICATIONS:
WHY HAVING ADD, NLD or ASD PROVIDES ADDITIONAL CHALLENGES!

If you have been diagnosed with ADD, NLD or an ASD, you may find that you have difficulty gaining the sense that you do, indeed, have choices. Truthfully, if you have ADD and you are not medicated, you will not have the choices you would have if you did take medication.

Medication used to treat ADD increases the overall flow of blood in the brain. At the same time, connections are smoother between the frontal cortex and the rest of the brain. Having a working connection to the frontal cortex is necessary for "executive functioning" such as planning, organizing, and making good decisions. If you choose not to take medications, you could be limiting your choices in other areas.

Of those diagnosed with borderline personality disorder, 37% also have ADD. Therefore, it makes sense that there is so much overlap in symptomology.[92] The co-occurrence rate (of ADD with) Asperger's Disorder (AS) or Pervasive Developmental Disorder- Not Otherwise Specified (PDD-NOS) was 85%. This was significantly higher than for (Kanner's Type) Autistic Disorder (57.6 %.)[93] Therefore, this expanded section may apply to those diagnosed with either BPD or with AS who have never considered ADD as an additional possibility.

Step Twelve
Intensity Is A Choice

When I had nothing,
You were something.
I opened my arms,
You closed my mind.
When I had been healing,
You promised danger.
When my soul was remorseful,
You promised pain.
When I had no one,
You were some one.
When I needed salvation,
You pulled me in deep.
When I had something I needed within,
You were nothing—
So I closed you off from my life, and I left you,
Alone, in your danger and pain,
Wishing you had something,
Were something, someone again.

Vampires are 100% real- in a metaphorical sense, of course. There are forces in their lives that people diagnosed with BPD (and often ADD) feel inexorably drawn to, dangerous forces which keep their lives in constant turbulence and uncertainty. Human beings, such as "sociopaths," collective groups of people, such as cults, and substances such as alcohol, food and drugs, and experiences, such as sex, shopping, gambling or reckless driving keep the adrenaline pumping, the senses feeling alive.

The person with BPD listens to a quiet voice, like the cartoon angel sitting on one shoulder that says, "No, this is not a good idea," but then finds herself driven by curiosity, stunned by the force of her emotions in reaction to the object, person or experience until all clear thinking is overwhelmed in a hypnotic craving to do this action. The experience, person, or object begins to sap their energy as though it is draining blood from them.

Soon, they become like "zombies" or "walking dead" in response to it. They feel empty without "it," feel powerless to avoid "it," and the power to choose is gone. The person with BPD may feel emotionally and spiritually dead. In the vampire movies, victims often hold up a cross or holy water or another sort of holy relic to ward the vampires away. Instinctively, the victims know to call upon a symbolic power of goodness and life. The victims have discovered a very primitive "higher power" that works in the story.

Am I describing addictive behavior or borderline behavior? I am describing neither and I am describing both. It is the style and motivations for the behavior described above that differentiates the borderline from the non-borderline addict. It is the frequency and intensity of giving in to harmful urges that separates the normal from the pathological, I believe.

Not all persons who behave as I've described above are addicts. In the examples above, I explained human behavior much more than any one sort of pathological type of behavior. We are all "led into temptation" at one time or another. To me, it is the level of intensity and frequency of giving into these urges which is relevant, as well as the patterns involved.

For example, people diagnosed with BPD tend to grab whatever is closest in the immediate environment to cling to in a time of need, whether that be a fifth of Jack Daniels or a blind date with someone from the classified ads. A non-borderline addict is more driven in one direction for extended periods of time. His addiction may change over the years from cocaine to heroin, for instance, but he is less likely to be as indiscriminate as the true borderline in deciding what can fill his needs... unless, of course, he has many borderline traits.

People diagnosed with BPD are often fascinated with being overpowered, as frightening as this may be. The non-borderline addict, on the other hand, tends to be obsessed with control, approaching "the vampire" with an attitude of, "I can conquer you." For example, whereas the addict wants to prove to himself that he can handle living on the edge and taking large quantities of drugs to feel powerful and able to take on the world, I believe the borderline is more like a woman being seduced by a vampire. She is wanting to surrender to a power greater than herself, to be helpless and therefore not in control of or responsible for her actions.

Since "being borderline" and having addictive disease are not mutually exclusive, she could benefit from a twelve step program and developing a relationship with a higher power. The concept of powerlessness to a borderline, however, often is a "no-brainer."

For years, whenever I have seen a scary movie or horror film, such as *Aliens* or *Cape Fear*, I have instinctually "known" that even though the villain or predator appears to be dead, it is, in fact, not. While those around me breathe a sigh of relief, believing the nightmare is over, I am alert, waiting for the evil thing to rise again. This is an instinctive reaction, similar to the experience of living with borderline personality disorder.

Just when she believes the nightmare is over, just when she believes her life is stable and back on track, and peace of mind and stability of emotions is emerging, watch out! Along comes the soul ravaging beast from within, presenting her with too much emotion, too much intensity, too much confusion, and too much need for any human being to easily sustain.

So often, I've thought of this illness as a continuous nightmare, as the periods of calm between episodes cannot be fully enjoyed, because they seem to be "the calm before the storm," which inevitably comes. It is no wonder that persons suffering from BPD so often plead to be saved from themselves. I believe people diagnosed with BPD understand danger as few other human beings do. They become obsessed with keeping themselves safe in reaction to the danger they have experienced. They wonder why their lives have been so full of "close calls" and "near misses." People diagnosed with BPD live out the intensity they feel inside, also instinctively.

Through therapy, it is possible to learn that this intensity is a choice. The chaos within does not necessarily need to be lived out to be resolved. Yet, before this realization is reached, people diagnosed with BPD feed on intensity to survive. Intensity tells them that they are alive, which may not have been perceived before. Since perception constitutes reality, people diagnosed with BPD honestly believe that they cannot live without intense experiences.

EXPANDED APPLICATIONS:

Coincidentally, people with ADD live out an almost identical dynamic. In fact, those with ADD usually organize their lives around thrilling experiences and situations. In other words, the thrills (including even terrifying experiences,) actually structure reality for many people who have attention deficit disorder. When one's attention is continually drifting, intense moments have one incredible effect: They make the drifting stop. It's no wonder so many with ADD are addicted to thrill-seeking behavior. As with any addiction, people with ADD can also practice reminding themselves that intensity is a choice for them as well.

A Warning About Relationships To Avoid

I'm about to mention a very intense experience which I can assure you, you can live without. You have enough intensity within yourself at times, (which presents a danger to your mental and emotional stability) without adding threats to your physical survival as well.

Antisocial Personality Disorders

People diagnosed with BPD (and often ADD) are often drawn to them like magnets, compelled by a powerful intensity of excitement, apparent connectedness and intrigue. Who are these people? They have engaged in quite a variety of criminal behavior. Crime to the antisocial is as self-destructiveness is to the BPD. This is what propels each illness, and, as these two begin to tango, the dance of destruction is the inevitable result.

The person diagnosed with BPD who can recognize the antisocial and then have the strength to avoid him has protected herself from danger far beyond heartbreak. He is often highly intelligent, charming, and a good conversationalist. He may know a great deal about a variety of subjects.

As you begin to talk further, you realize that he has a criminal history which he may try to minimize, saying such things as, "Yeah, I've been arrested six times, but I never did any time for any of them" or, "Yes, I've had three DUI's and two battery charges but I was only violent when I drank and I don't drink any more." You are so taken in by his charm and affections that you really want to see his point, because wouldn't it be great if he really is a reformed rascal and not a manipulative, lying con?

Anything he says you really want to forgive and overlook, because, after all, he is so good to you right now. It doesn't matter that he just told you that he tried to kill his mother when he was fourteen, or that he once had sexual relations with a thirteen year old. He has told you, with tears in his eyes, how desperate and confused he was and how all he needed then was love.

How amazing! That's all you ever needed too, and you have also done your share of crazy things to get love. You embrace and feel that you understand one another.

Time for a reality shock. If you don't realize this now, it will slap you hard in the face later:

This interaction you are having is DECEPTIVE. This is not the deep love and connectedness you have always dreamed of. This is a SUPERFICIAL MANIPULATION by him, and an act of DESPERATION by you. WHY? you ask, perhaps angrily.

Because intensity does not equal love. Because personality disorders are categorized by the inability to love and be loved and to form satisfactory relationships. The perfect chemistry you are looking at is volatile. **Two half persons do not make a whole.**

As I've worked with "borderline" clients, I've watched the majority, one by one, become caught up in relationships with antisocial personality disordered men. I've watched the drama so many times that it is like a sad re-run on television. I don't think that writing this and sending this message out in print will do much at all to solve the problem. Many readers will not believe me.

Many readers are currently in these types of relationships and are afraid of being alone and feeling abandoned if they were to transfer themselves to safety. But, maybe one of you will have a moment of realization that the relationship you are in will not work out successfully. And, if he doesn't manipulate you into taking him back, my keying this message into my computer will be well worth the time.

People diagnosed with BPD often place themselves in the position of victim in relationships, and are even prone to have masochistic motivations for this. This pattern of behavior can stop NOW. If you are in a relationship with a controlling man, abusive man, or a man you don't quite trust, then TRUST YOURSELF and find another plan for your life. And, if you are not in a relationship now, and you see or meet these men, think of them as a seven layer chocolate cake with poison in every layer, and think to yourself, "No, Thank you, I don't think I'll be the victim of a dashing looking Dracula today."

EXPANDED APPLICATIONS:
Incidentally, those diagnosed with ADD, NLD or ASD's tend to be drawn into relationships with those diagnosed with BPD. This is also NOT a winning combination. If you find that you are suffering more than enjoying your relationship, consider moving on. Many people with neurological conditions have reported feeling abused by those with BPD. Please realize that this is NOT their actual intent. However, I felt it was necessary to include the "reverse" type of warning that relationships with BPDs may not necessarily be healthy or compatible with your type of difficulty.

Angst (written 10/3/92)

There's a jester with a gavel
and he's banging on my head
The courtroom is a courtyard
where wildflowers grow
in the jury box
where my thoughts stop
at the cortex of my skull
and there is silence
anticipation
for the sentencing
like a period. STOP.
I suck my breath in. hold.
I can not testify.
There are no witnesses.
The judge stands on his head
as his beard and his bells hide his face.
The court will come to disorder
as the gloomy eyed ghosts
show their envelope to His Honor
who asks me whether I will escape again
I said I never know if I ever do
and he said STOP and you can GO.

Resiliency and Relapse Prevention

Jerold Kreisman, M.D. and Hal Straus wrote
about the borderline society in the popular and
informative book, *I Hate You-Don't Leave Me,
Understanding the Borderline Personality*. In this
book, they addressed the disintegrating culture,
breakdown of structure, a fragmented society, dread
of the future, jungle of interpersonal relationships,
shifting gender role patterns, and shifting family and
child rearing patterns. All of these factors, the authors
assert, tend to aggravate the pathological response to
these stressors known as the borderline syndrome.
The book states that "borderline traits, which may be

present, to some extent in most people, are being elicited, perhaps even bred, on a wide scale by the prevailing social conditions" [94]

This brings us to the point of view that one diagnosed with BPD has of survival. Again, I quote from the Kreisman-Strauss book referenced above:

Empirical studies with adolescents and children have consistently shown awareness of the danger of nuclear annihilation, hopelessness about surviving, a shortened time perspective, and pessimism about being able to reach life goals. Suicide is mentioned again and again as a strategy for dealing with the threat.

Later, he states:

With little interest in the past, the borderline is almost a cultural amnesiac; his cupboard of warm memories (which sustain most of us in troubled times) is bare. As a result, he is doomed to suffer torment, with no breathers, no concrete memories of happier times to get him through the tough periods. Unable to learn from his mistakes, he is doomed to repeat them. [95]

This torment in troubled times, combined with inner intensity of emotion, not modulated or comforted, leads to even less assurance of survival for vulnerable people. They cannot simply "walk away" from threatening and overwhelming emotions within their own bodies, much less from external threat and stressors facing them.

However, this passage assumes that those diagnosed with BPD have been traumatized and have difficulty recalling positive childhood memories. Also, people who have right hemisphere brain dysfunction syndromes also have great difficulty learning from mistakes, generalizing to new situations and gaining enough encouragement after a history of repeated failures to try again. In fact, any suicidal person may be suffering from "insufficiency of the right hemisphere:

> It is suggested that due to functional insufficiency of the right hemisphere, the suicidal person demonstrates a compensatory shift to left hemisphere functioning. This shift manifests itself in reversed asymmetry of neurotransmitters, tendency to dissociation, alienated and negative perception of the body, lower sensitivity to pain, disintegration of self-representation, cognitive constriction, overly general nature of personal memories, difficulties in affect regulation as well as such personality traits as low openness to experience and personal constriction. [96]

The psychologist Judith Herman, PhD, had found "documented histories of severe childhood trauma in the great majority (81%) of cases" of borderline personality).[97] She had also found that "the earlier the onset of abuse and the greater its severity, the greater the likelihood that the survivor would develop symptoms of borderline personality disorder." 81% might be considered rather high.

More recent studies have shown reported abuse as between 40-60%. In addition, the 2003 study by Dr. Golier concluded that "results do not appear substantial or distinct enough to support singling out BPD from other personality disorders or as a trauma based disorder or variant of PTSD."[98] Also, a 2006 study did not support the hypothesis that childhood sexual abuse is directly related to the neurobiological abnormalities found in BPD.[99]

Regardless of whether BPD traits are acquired through environmental trauma, biological disposition, or both, methods used to cope with this high intensity emotional response to stressors have often been very successful. Pharmaceutically, drug agents such as lithium, (primarily used in bipolar disorder), and depakote, (formerly used only with seizures, and later used to control mania and impulsivity) have been used increasingly in the treatment of borderline patients, to modulate emotional intensity, impulsivity, and agitation.

Anti-psychotic drugs are also used occasionally to treat these symptoms when other drugs are found to be ineffective, and to help the borderline to cope through micro-psychotic episodes. Anti-depressants are used when the primary symptoms indicate clinical depression, as when the person diagnosed with BPD has felt intensely sad and/or empty and full of malaise for an extended period of time. Increasingly, anti-depressants such as Prozac or Zoloft have been used to treat BPD, regardless of whether clinical depression is present.

Zoloft (now available under generic names, such as seratraline) is actually the only proven effective treatment for PTSD, so if you are a person who does have a history of trauma, consider specifically asking for Zoloft for this reason.[100]

Dialectical Behavior Therapy (DBT) has been used with some measure of success with borderline personality disorder. The DBT program includes "classes" in coping skills and emotional modulation in addition to the individual therapy sessions, which, in my opinion, is a clear strength of this approach.

Even though dialectic behavior therapy has been proven to be an effective approach, remember that it is the skill and competence of the practitioner that makes the difference, not merely the technique or orientation used. As referenced in earlier chapters, cognitive behavioral therapy and psychodynamic therapy have both proven effectiveness in recent years.

The most important factor in recovery, I believe, is to stay dedicated to the process of recovery, through good times and bad. Many therapists now favor long-term intermittent supportive therapy for BPD. This type of therapy means therapy only in times of crisis, which is the typical pattern people diagnosed with BPD often follow when they aren't aware of the benefits of sticking with long-term treatment.

Many therapists also believe that BPD will go away on its own as the individuals suffering from it grow and mature. There does seem to be some substance to this theory, as persons diagnosed with BPD often "mellow out" or achieve a sort of equilibrium in middle age.

My viewpoint is that in some instances, staying consistently in psychotherapy could prevent problems from ever becoming crises in the first place. Also, although people diagnosed with BPD seem to "mellow out" with age, this is not always the case. I believe that psychotherapy can improve the quality of life for people diagnosed with BPD, whether they are currently in crisis or not.

Equally important is to have access to a good psychiatrist if the primary therapist is a psychologist or social worker. Rachel Reiland recovered from BPD after meeting several times a week with her psychiatrist, for both psychotherapy and medication management, over a number of years. However, having a psychiatrist for medication management and a separate psychotherapist is often the best idea, for this gives the patient two different professionals to turn to in a crisis, so that if one of them is indisposed, there is still someone for the patient diagnosed with BPD to contact.

Equally essential is to have some form of therapy group, support group, or network of persons to turn to in a crisis, because such a system diffuses over-dependency on one person, who would likely to become overburdened and burned out regardless of his skill in limit setting with such a patient. Social networking lowers the intensity of dependency, and that strength serves to mitigate the strong and overwhelming feelings of abandonment and emptiness (which some, but not all people diagnosed with BPD experience.) Through regular contact with a support network, much of the associated acting-out behaviors can often be modulated or even avoided entirely.

Therapists can assist in the process of teaching emotional modulation by intentionally showing the patient how to control the intensity level of emotional experiences. Therapists can also assist the patient by trying to keep the sessions on a low to moderate level of intensity.

In a study by LaNae Valentine, Ph.D and Leslie L. Feinauer, Ph.D.,[101] women who endured childhood sexual abuse without apparent psychological harm shared certain characteristics. They had a network of social support beyond the family, they thought well of themselves, did not blame themselves, and they had a sense of spirituality and of taking charge of their own lives. If you have endured trauma, or if you have merely become despondent because no treatment has resolved your symptoms, the above information is useful to remember in order to cope more effectively with your life today.

Drs. Robert Brooks and Sam Goldstein, authors of *Raising Resilient Children*,[102] outline the keys they have observed to the "resilient mindset" of children who overcome adversity without developing significant psychological problems. The first is the ability to, "Define what one has control over and focus one's time and energy on these areas."

This simple statement is reminiscent of AA's "serenity prayer," which states, "God, give me the serenity to accept what I cannot change, the courage to change the things I can, and the wisdom to know the difference."

The Importance of Practicing Coping Skills

When a person desires physical strength and fitness, she often undertakes an exercise regimen. When a person desires emotional strength and fitness, what is there to do? Most psycho-educational groups in hospitals and outpatient treatment facilities teach coping skills, either through a group exercise, lecture, or discussion group. Many group leaders have an agenda before group starts to cover a certain amount of material, similar to the agenda used in many intellectual classes.

I believe that psycho-educational groups work best when the format of the group is practical, focused toward the individual, and presented in a manner of practice exercises rather than as a steady stream of information which is directed primarily to the intellectual faculties of the client. Would the client wish for more emotional strength and fitness or for an intellectual understanding of skills which he or she may or may not be able to use? Many therapists feel that outside the psycho-ed group is the best format for practicing coping skills, when the stressors present themselves from the outside. I disagree. This way of thinking is comparable to teaching a physical fitness class in the following way:

The coach speaks before his team about strategies to cope with situations which might present themselves on the playing field. In a "baseball class," he reads the team a list of ways to handle these situations, and asks the team, "Which of these could you apply at the next ball game?" A pitcher speaks up. He says, "Well, if I see a batter like the one you described, I would throw him a curve ball." The "coach" asks the pitcher if he understands how to throw a curve ball, the pitcher carefully reads the directions on the xeroxed copy he is holding, and says, "I guess so."

Is this player in any way prepared for the game? Wouldn't it be better if the player could practice throwing this pitch in a mock game situation before the game? Otherwise, to continue our analogy, the pitcher goes to play against another team (just as the clients in a psycho-educational group go to play in the fields of their own personal lives), and he will probably not even remember the description of the pitch he read about because he never had an opportunity to practice it with support and direction of a coach, or to use the information at all. Unless the player is a "natural," the time he spent in this baseball class has been wasted. How many mental health clients are "naturals" at using coping skills?

My thesis is that knowledge by itself never saved anyone. An example of this is a television advertisement which shows a diner choking at the table. The people at his table are discussing the Heimlich maneuver, but nobody helps him except someone from another table, who never says a word. Just because you can explain how to bake a cake doesn't mean you can actually do it. Just because you tell your therapist you understand how to "create new scenarios" to help you to make more positive decisions does not mean you can do it.

Therapists expect clients to practice in their own lives outside of group and bring the experiences they have had, positive or negative, back to the group situation. This is good, but my belief is that a group is more productive if one coping skill has been taught and practiced in the group so that it can be easily implemented outside of group than if twelve or even twenty have been presented and merely discussed. I believe psycho-educational groups should follow more of a physical fitness model in these respects than that of an "educational" format.

Because I believe this, I offer a program of exercises which do far more than teach an idea or concept. They strengthen and develop skills, as good coaches do muscles. These should be practiced on a regular basis until they become second nature, whether in a group setting, within individual therapy sessions, or on your own. At the end of this chapter are a few useful exercises which may aid in the process.

Relapse and Resiliency

There is a story of Winnie the Poo, written by A.A. Milne,[103] about a problem that occurs in which Eeyore has had a very rough time, having slipped down a river bank. When Rabbit and Roo asked him how he managed to fall down, he stated that he was bounced. He insisted that he didn't slip and it wasn't an accident. He had been bounced by Tigger.

So, then, Rabbit decided that the thing to do was to "unbounce Tigger" with a cruel plan in which the three would take Tigger far into the forest where Tigger had never been before and leave him there, lost, alone and abandoned, until he would become a "sad and sorry Tigger," who would bounce no more. But ironically, rather than Tigger becoming lost, Rabbit became lost, although Pooh and Piglet found their way back after a while. All of the animals watched Tigger frantically yapping until finally, Rabbit felt sorry for himself because he was lost and ran out to greet Tigger. At that moment, Tigger bounced happily and Rabbit appreciated Tigger's bounce again, since Tigger was able to help him to find the way home.

This wonderful ironic story illustrates exactly why we should not try to "un-bounce" or "un-borderline" ourselves. The same parts of us that push others down and away from ourselves can be grand, friendly, large and helpful as well. The same parts. The violence we turn on ourselves can be the driving passion of our lives to improve, rather than to self-destruct. It's the Edward Scissorhands fable all over again, only rather than scissors, here we have bounce. And, speaking of bounce, herein lies a secret of survival- resiliency, which is why this story was chosen. Like Tigger, people diagnosed with BPD have bounced people down and bounced them back home. The catch here is that you need that very bounce to get back on track. It is too easy to surrender to hopelessness and feelings of futility. A person without resiliency is a person on her way to the cemetery. Just as in addictions therapy, "relapses" are part of the recovery process, not the end of it, if they are approached correctly, with questions such as:

1. What have I learned from this?
2. What were the triggers (pardon the look-alike word) that led to the relapse of negative behavior?
3. Are there any amends that need to be made?
4. Are there any changes in my lifestyle that need to be made to prevent such an occurrence from happening again?
5. What can I do differently in this situation if it happens again?

Following such an evaluation, an attempt to get back on track should occur as soon as possible. Try to think of healthy and positive things to do which can help you to feel better about yourself, such as playing a musical instrument, cleaning up a room, doing some writing or gardening or any activity which gives you a positive sense of accomplishment upon completion.

Focus on your positives, not your negatives. If you are surrounded by negative people who continue to complain bitterly and bring up the relapse behavior, avoid them as much as possible. Check other sections of this program for self-comforting tips and activities to modulate intense emotions. As long as you are working in this program, you are healing from your illness. Continue to move forward. No work toward healing is ever lost unless you die. Everything you do towards your own healing work is valuable. Soon, you will get your "bounce" back and hop back on the right track. Other people will be glad to see you. Sometimes they are feeling "sad and sorry" about other things and all they need is to see you again, their passionately affectionate and helpful friend.

Appendix,

Acknowledgements,

Endnotes

Appendix I
General Recommendation: In the instances below, I refer to the treating professional as "doctor." Your primary treatment professional may be a PhD psychologist or master's level therapist. If your primary difficulty is BPD, these may be good choices for you. However, I have found the best results from one hour of weekly therapy with an M.D, PhD, who is more able to manage the biochemical aspects of treatment along with therapeutic issues. For me, the best part about working with an M.D. is that my medical doctor can fluently move between neurological underpinnings for behavior that need to be treated with medication and my separate behavioral issues that I can control myself.

Rachel Reiland, who also recovered successfully from BPD also received treatment with an M.D. Her treatment was 2-3 times per week for several years. My consulting clients who choose an M.D. as primary "treater" also seem to do much better. If you have accompanying neurological disabilities or suspect that you do, and a good M.D. psychotherapist is unavailable, a neuropsychologist (specialized PhD) might also be a good choice for you.

General Guidelines for Patients Who Have Been Diagnosed With BPD:

(1) Make sure that professionals have ruled out every other possible cause or diagnosis first.

(2) If you have neurological issues, don't back down if they are ignored or dismissed. Seek an advocate if possible. If the root of my difficulties had been properly evaluated and treated, I might not have had to work so hard and put my body through so much physical stress for ten years. So, I hope others may not needlessly suffer as I did.

(3) Don't necessarily take this diagnosis very seriously. BPD is considered a very serious mental illness. But, that doesn't mean you need to move into feeling dramatic about how severely "screwed up" you are, and how your future is doomed to failure. You decide how you are going to live your life and create your future, not a doctor.

(4) A good doctor can still help you a great deal through your recovery process. Choose carefully. Do you usually feel secure and "contained" when you are in his office? Do you feel that he or she has genuine empathy for your struggles and needs? Do you sense that your treating professional is seeing you as a person first, and as a "diagnosis" second?

(5) Take full responsibility for doing your best to change your beliefs and behaviors. Refrain from "victim thinking" or blaming others, as this will affect you like poison and invariably make your condition worse.

(6) If you sense that your doctor is not consistently conveying a positive message that you are capable of making movement in therapy, you either need to find a new doctor or take a hard look at how "victim thinking" may be holding you back from taking more responsibility for your recovery.

Appendix II
COMPARE/CONTRAST CHART

TRAIT	BPD	ASD
Emotional developmental delay	Yes	Yes
Often accused of "having no empathy"	Yes	Yes
Intense emotional "meltdowns"	Yes	Yes
Self-Mutilation	Often	Often
Difficulty with construct of "identity."	Yes	Yes
Concrete and "black and white" thinking**	Yes	Yes
Areas of the Brain Most Relevant	Limbic System (Amygdala, Hippocampus) and Frontal Cortex	Limbic System (Amygdala, Hippocampus) and Frontal Cortex
Reduced hippocampus volume	Yes- 16% smaller[104] [105] reduced volume[106]	Yes- Reduced hippocampus volume[107] Larger LEFT Hippocampal Volume[108]
*Reduced amygdala volume	Yes-7.5% smaller [109] [110] 8% smaller[111] Amygdala hyperreactivity[112] "abnormal"	Yes-Less LEFT amygdala volume[114] Reduced overall amygdala volume[115]

	amygdala[113]	
Pre-Frontal Cortex Abnormalities	Abnormalities in pre-frontal cortex[116] Low level brain activity and deficiency of serotonin in pre-frontal cortex.[117] reduction in frontal and orbito-frontal lobe volumes[118] [119] Neuropsychological testing implied a dysfunction in the right hemisphere frontotemporal region in BPD individuals.[120] There was a significant 24% reduction of the left orbitofrontal and a 26% reduction of the right anterior cingulate gyrus[121]	Strong evidence supporting one of the major theories of autism, known as the limbic system theory, which suggests that damage to the amygdala and the frontal cortex contributes highly to what appears to be the primary symptom of autism, social impairment.[122]
Often relate better to animals or children	Yes	Yes
Prone to regression under stress	Yes	Yes

"Expected" Presentation	Dramatic, "Histrionic"	Often flat, speaking in monotone
Gender usually diagnosed	Females	Males
Usually Resolves by Age 35-50	Yes	No
The Case for Genetics/Heredity	35% MZ twins; 7% DZ twins[123]	92% MZ twins; 10% DZ twins; (but DZ rate is over 200x general population rate)[124]

Key: BPD (Borderline Personality Disorder)
ASD (Autistic Spectrum Disorder)

Notes:
*The amygdala is associated with socioemotional function and has been implicated in the pathophysiology of autism.[125]

**"Someone with a nonverbal learning disability will be very concrete in terms of black and white, true and false."
-Sue Thompson, M.A., C.E.T., author of *The Source for Nonverbal Learning Disorders.*

ACKNOWLEDGEMENTS:

I'd once again like to thank my former husband, John Paxton, my departed mother, Dr. Thelma Hall, my father Dr. Wilson Hall, Dr. Robert Paisley, former therapist and the also recently departed Professor Collie Owens, for their assistance with the original edition of *Borderline and Beyond.* In this third revision, my father served as the main editor. His continual unconditional love and support has served as an anchor for me throughout my life. I want to thank him for believing in me, no matter what, 100%.

I also want to express my deepest thanks to each professional who treated or assessed me during the past year, including Glenn Cahn, PhD; James Byassee, PhD; The North Carolina Autism Society, and especially Shelley Moore, adult group faciliator; my occupational therapist Saundra Newton, OTR/L; Neurologist Ataif Hussain, M.D.; ASD Consultant Mark Moffet, M.D.; and especially Lynn David Ikenberry, M.D., Ph.D, who has had a major impact and influence on this book through providing my primary care this year.

Borderline and Beyond Consulting Services

Laura Paxton is available for workshops and presentations for hospitals, clinics and mental health centers. Laura is also available for inspirational talks for patients who are suffering from severe emotional illness or autism. She also offers phone and internet counseling and consulting on a limited basis through http://www.laurapaxton.com. For more information, e-mail Laura@LauraPaxton.com.

154 Laura Paxton

ENDNOTES

[1] M. Linehan et al, Cognitive-behavioral treatment of chronically parasuicidal borderline patients. *Arch Gen Psychiatry* 1991 Dec;48(12):1060-4.

[2] CA Binks, M Fenton, L McCarthy, T Lee, CE Adams, C Duggan, "Psychological therapies for people with borderline personality disorder," *The Cochrane Database of Systematic Reviews* 2006, Issue 1. Art. No.: CD005652. DOI: 10.1002/14651858.CD005652.

[3] Russell Meares, Janine Stevenson, & Anne Comerford, (1999) "Psychotherapy with borderline patients: I. A comparison between treated and untreated cohorts." *Australian and New Zealand Journal of Psychiatry* 33 (4), 467-472.

[4] Neil Walker, Margaret Whelan, "Survey of Sensory Problems in 30 Autistic Adults and Children," Cited in *Thinking in Pictures: My Life with Autism* by Temple Grandin, Vintage Books, 1995.

5 S. Parush, 1994: "Dissertation subject: Behavioral and Electrophysiological Correlates of Attention Deficit Hyperactivity Disorder with and without Tactile Defensiveness" Under the guidance of Prof. H. Sohmer (physiology) and Dr. M. Kaitz (psychology). Dissertation was published in the Journal: *Developmental Medicine and Child Neurology*, 1997, 39, 464-46.

6 Hagop S Akiskal, "Die borderline-persönlichkeit: affektive grundlagen symptome und syndrome (Borderline personality: affective substrates, symptoms, and syndromes,)" In: Kernberg OF, Dulz B, Sachsse U, eds. Handbuch der Borderline-Störungen. Stuttgart: Schattauer, 2000: 259–270.

7 N Nehls, "Borderline personality disorder: the voice of patients," Res Nurs Health 1999;22: 285–293.

8 Hagop S Akiskal, (2004) "Demystifying borderline personality: critique of the concept and unorthodox reflections on its natural kinship with the bipolar spectrum," Acta Psychiatrica Scandinavica 110 (6), 401-407. doi: 10.1111/j.1600-0447.2004.00461.x

[9] MF Lenzenweger, "Stability and change in personality disorder features: the Longitudinal Study of Personality Disorders." *Arch Gen Psychiatry* 56(11):1009-1015. (1999.)

[10]MC Zanarini, FR Frankenburg, J Hennen, KR Silk, "The longitudinal course of borderline psychopathology: 6-year prospective follow-up of the phenomenology of borderline personality disorder," Am J Psychiatry 160(2):274-283. (2003.)
[11] John M. Oldham, M.D., "Borderline Personality Disorder: An Overview," *Psychiatric Times,* July, 2004. Volume xx1, Issue 8.
[12] Roger Peele, "Should BPD be on Axis I? Understanding the Issue: Summary of the Debate with Roger Peele, M.D. and John Oldham, M.D.," 2003 American Psychiatric Association Annual Meeting, San Francisco, CA.
[13] Valerie Porr, "How Advocacy is Bringing Borderline Personality Disorder Into the Light," *TEN: The Economics of Neuroscience,* November, 2001.
[14] TARA APD=Treatment and Research Advancement Association for Personality Disorders. (www.tara4bpd.org)
[15] J.A Dvoskin,"Sticks and Stones – The abuse of psychiatric diagnosis in prisons," www.vachss.com/guest_dispatches/dvoskin.html, accessed August 3, 2002.
[16] Bienenfeld, E-Medicine On-line Dictionary, March, 2006 Created by eMedicine.com and the National Center for Medical Informatics.
[17] G Perugi, C Toni, MC Travierso, HS Akiskal, ELSEVIER SCIENCE BV, PO BOX 211, 1000 AE AMSTERDAM, NETHERLANDS JAN 2003, The role of cyclothymia in atypical depression: toward a data-based reconceptualization of the borderline-bipolar II connection, JOURNAL OF AFFECTIVE DISORDERS 73 (1-2): 87-98.
[18] (1994, July) Borderline Personality Disorder-Part III, Harvard Mental Health Letter.
[19] Ibid.
[20]American Psychiatric Association. October, 2001. Practice Guideline for Treatment of Patients with Borderline Personality Disorder.
http://www.psych.org/psych_pract/treatg/pg/borderline_reviseb ook_index.cfm
[21] Rachel Reiland, *I'm Not Supposed to Be Here*, Eggshells Press, 2002.

[22] Rachel Reiland, *Get Me Out of Here: My Recovery from Borderline Personality Disorder*, Hazelden, 2004.

[23] N.R. Bockian, *New Hope for People with Borderline Personality Disorder,*. Prima Publishing, Rosville, Calfornia, 2002. 26.

[24] Andrew E. Skodol, M.D., et al. "The Borderline Diagnosis: Psychopathology, Co-Morbidity, and Personality Structure," *Biological Psychiatry in Press*, Elsevier Science, Inc., 2002.

[25] Julia A. Golier, M.D., Rachel Yehuda, Ph.D., Linda M. Bierer, M.D., Vivian Mitropoulou, M.A., Antonia S. New, M.D., James Schmeidler, Ph.D., Jeremy M. Silverman, Ph.D. and Larry J. Siever, M.D., "The Relationship of Borderline Personality Disorder to Posttraumatic Stress Disorder and Traumatic Events," Am J Psychiatry 160:2018-2024, November 2003.

[26] K Lieb, M Zanarini, C Schmahl, M Linehan, M. Bohus, "Borderline Personality Disorder," *The Lancet*, 2004; 364:453-61. July 21, 2004.

[27] Julia A. Golier, M.D., Rachel Yehuda, Ph.D., Linda M. Bierer, M.D., Vivian Mitropoulou, M.A., Antonia S. New, M.D., James Schmeidler, Ph.D., Jeremy M. Silverman, Ph.D. and Larry J. Siever, M.D., *"The Relationship of Borderline Personality Disorder to Posttraumatic Stress Disorder and Traumatic Events,"* Am J Psychiatry 160:2018-2024, November 2003.

[28]Tess Wilkinson-Ryan, A.B., and Drew Westen, Ph.D., *Identity Disturbance in Borderline Personality Disorder: An Empirical Investigation*, 2000.

[29] Hagop S. Akiskal, (2004) "Demystifying borderline personality: critique of the concept and unorthodox reflections on its natural kinship with the bipolar spectrum," *Acta Psychiatrica Scandinavica* 110 (6), 401-407. doi: 10.1111/j.1600-0447.2004.00461.x.

[30] Ibid.

[31] N Atre-Vaida, SM Hussain, Borderline Personality Disorder and Bipolar Mood Disorder: Two Distinct Disorders or a Continuum? J Nervous & Mental Disorders, 1999, 187: 3 13-5.

[32]Hagop S. Akiskal, Invited Guest Editor, "Demystifying borderline personality: critique of the concept and unorthodox reflections on its natural kinship with the bipolar spectrum," Acta Psychiatrica Scandinavica, *Acta Psychiatrica Scandinavica* 2004 110:6 401.

[33] PR Joyce, RT Mulder, SE Luty, JM Mckenzie, PF Sullivan, RC Cloninger, "Borderline personality disorder in major depression: symptomatology, temperament, character,

differential drug response, and 6-month outcome," *Compr Psychiatry* 2003;44: 35–43.

[34]R Bloink, P Brieger, HS Akiskal, A.Marneros, "Factorial structure and internal consistency of the German TEMPS-A scale: validation against the NEO-FFI questionnaire," *J Affect Disord* 2004.

[35]JG Gunderson, I Weinberg, MT Daversa, KD Kueppenbender, MC Zanarini, MT Shea, A E Skodol AE, C A Sanislow, S Yen, LC Morey, CM Grilo, TH McGlashan, RL Stout, I Dyck. *Descriptive and longitudinal observations on the relationship of borderline personality disorder and bipolar disorder.* Am J Psychiatry. 2006 Jul;163(7):1126-8.

[36] Leanne M. Williams, M.D, Anna Sidis, M.D.; Evian Gordon, M.D. and Russell A. Meares, M.D., May 2006 study: "Missing Links in Borderline Personality Disorder: Loss of Neural Synchrony Relates to Lack of Emotional Regulation and Impulse Control," *Psychiatry Neuroscience,* 2006 May; 31(3): 181–188.

[37] Ibid.

[38]Tess Wilkinson-Ryan, A.B., and Drew Westen, Ph.D., "Identity Disturbance in Borderline Personality Disorder: An Empirical Investigation," 2000

[39] Michael Jonathan Grinfeld, Conference Probes Pathology of Self-Awareness. Psychiatric Times, Volume XX. Issue 6. June, 2003.

[40] Jerold J. Kreisman & Hal Strauss, (1989) *I Hate You-Don't Leave Me: Understanding the Borderline Personality,* New York: Avon Books.

[41] *The BC Early Intervention Study, CMHA BC Division.* 1998.

[42] Lydia Lewis, Executive Director DBSA, "The Face of Bipolar Illness," Presented at American Psychiatric Association Annual Meeting, May, 2001.

[43] Linda M. McLean, PhD and Ruth Gallop, "Implications of Child Sexual Abuse for Adult BPD and Complex PTSD," American Journal of Psychiatry, 160 (2) 396-71.

[44] Jeannette LeGris, BN, MHSc, PhD Candidate, Rob van Reekum, MD, FRCPC, "The Neuropsychological Correlates of Borderline Personality Disorder and Suicidal Behaviour," *Canadian Journal of Psychiatry.* 2006;51:131–142.

[45] Ibid.

[46] Robert van Reekum, M.D., Chris A Conway, M.D, David Gansler, PhD, Roberta White PhD, David L Bachman, M.D., *Neurobehavioral Study of Borderline Personality Disorder*, J Psychiatry Neuroscience, 1993 May; 18(3): 121-129.

[47] M Tohen, J Hennen, CM Zarate, et al., "Two Year Syndromal and Functional Recovery in 219 First Episode Cases of Major Affective Disorder with Psychotic Features," *Am J Psychiatry*, 2000; 157: 220-28.

[48] W Coryell, J Endicott, JD Maser, T Meuller, T Lavori, M. Keller, "The Likelihood of Recurrence of Bipolar Affective Disorder: The Importance of Episode Recency," *J Affect Disord*, 1995; 33: 201-06.

[49] K Lieb, M Zanarini, C Schmahl, M Linehan, M. Bohus, "Borderline Personality Disorder," *The Lancet*, 2004; 364:453-61. July 21, 2004.

[50] J Paris, H.Zweig-Frank , "A 27 year follow-up of patients with borderline personality disorder," *Compr Psychiatry* 2001;42:482-7.

[51] MC Zanarini, FR Frankenburg, J Hennen, KR Silk, "The longitudinal course of borderline psychopathology: 6-year prospective follow-up of the phenomenology of borderline personality disorder," *Am J Psychiatry* 2003;160:274-83.

[52] JG Gunderson, LC Morey, RL Stout, AE Skodol, MT Shea, TH McGlashan, et al., "Major depressive disorder and borderline personality disorder revisited: longitudinal interactions," *J Clin Psychiatry* 2004;65:1049-56.

[53] J Paris, H.Zweig-Frank, "A 27 year follow-up of patients with borderline personality disorder," *Compr Psychiatry* 2001;42:482-7.

[54] J. Paris, "Personality disorders over time," Washington: *American Psychiatric Press*; 2003.

[55] J. Paris, "Borderline Personality Disorder," *CMAJ*. 2005 Jun 7;172(12):1579-83

[56] G Perugi, C Toni, MC Travierso, HS Akiskal, the *JOURNAL OF AFFECTIVE DISORDERS: 2002.*

[57] Laith Farid Gulli M.D., Linda Hesson, M.A., Psy. S., LLP, CAC, Michael Mooney, M.A., CAC, CCS, "Borderline Personality Disorder," Encyclopedia of Mental Illness, *Minddisorders.com*, 2006.

[58] JM De la Fuente, "Neurologic Soft Signs in BPD," *Journal of Clinical Psychology*, 67 (4) 561-6. 2006.

[59] *The American Heritage® Stedman's Medical Dictionary*, 2nd Edition Copyright © 2004 by Houghton Mifflin Company.

[60] Leanne M. Williams, M.D, Anna Sidis, M.D.; Evian Gordon, M.D. and Russell A. Meares, M.D., May 2006 study: "Missing Links in Borderline Personality Disorder: Loss of Neural Synchrony Relates to Lack of Emotional Regulation and Impulse Control," *Psychiatry Neuroscience,* 2006 May; 31(3): 181–188.

[61] KIDS foundation SPD network on-line resource, http://www.sinetwork.org/

[62] *Gale Encyclopedia of Medicine*, Published December, 2002 by the Gale Group

[63] Sharon Heller, PhD, *Too Loud, Too Bright, Too Fast, Too Tight: What To Do If You Are Sensory Defensive in an Overstimulating World,* Harper Collins Publishers, Inc. New York, New York. (2003): 121.

[64] "Attention Deficit Disorder Hits Women Harder," says a May, 2005 article by Paula Moyer, published on *Med Page Today.*

[65] Ibid.

[66] Edward Hallowell, M.D. and John Ratey, M.D., *Driven to Distraction,* (1994) Simon & Schuster: New York.

[67] Ibid.

[68]Edwin H. Cook, Jr., et al., "Association of attention deficit disorder and the dopamine transporter gene," *American Journal of Human Genetics, 56,* 1995. Address: Edwin H. Cook, Jr., MC3077, 5841 South Maryland Avenue, Chicago, IL 60637.

[69] C Zlotnick ; L Rothschild ; M Zimmerman, "The role of gender in the clinical presentation of patients with borderline personality disorder," *J Personal Disord. 2002; 16(3):277-82* (ISSN: 0885-579X) Department of Psychiatry and Human Behavior, Box G-BH, Brown University, Providence, RI 02912, USA.

[70]DM Johnson, MT Shea, S Yen, CL Battle, C Zlotnick, CA Sanislow, CM Grilo, CM Skodol, AE Skodol, DX Bender, TH McGlashan, JG Gunderson, MC Zanarini, "Gender differences in borderline personality disorder: findings from the Collaborative longitudinal Personality Disorders Study," *Summa Health System*, St. Thomas Hospital, Akron, OH 44310, USA.

[71]Nicola Pytel, "Self-Injury Is Prevalent Among College Students," *Cornell University Research Press Release,* June 2006; summarizing Whitlock, J., Eckenrode, J. & Silverman, D. "Self-injurious Behaviors in a College Population" *Pediatrics* Vol. 117 No. 6 (June 2006) 1939-1948.

[72]"Helen Bonham Carter's Child Craving." *Softpedia News.* November, 2005. http://news.softpedia.com/news/Helena-Bonham-Carter-s-Child-Craving-12651.shtml.

[73] *Am J Psychiatry* 1987 Jun;144(6);748-52
"Sexual practices among patients borderline personality disorder."
("Homosexuality was 10 times more common among the men and six times more common among the women and borderline personality disorder than in the general population or in a depressed control group." Bisexuality and paraphilias were also relatively common.)

[74] Karen M Moore, MT, OTR/L, "Sensory Based Therapy: The Missing Piece in DBT," Presented at the MAOT-1998 Conference, 1998.

[75] Sharon Heller. *The Anxiety Myth: Why your anxiety may not be "All in Your Head" but from something physical*, Symmetry Publishing, Delray Beach, FL, 2006)
see: www.anxietymyth.com

[76] Ibid.

[77] Karen M Moore, MT, OTR/L and Alexis D Henry, ScD, OTR/L, "Treatment of Adult Psychiatric Patients Using the Wilbarger Protocol," 2002.

[78] P.L Travers, Mary Poppins. New York : Harcourt Brace Jovanovich, c1981.

[79] Diane Appleyard, *You Magazine*, "Did the Wrong Diet Make This Woman Autistic?" 1/19/1997.

[80] Rinne T, de Kloet ER, Wouters L, Goekoop JG, DeRijk RH, W van den Brink, "Hyperresponsiveness of hypothalamic-pituitary-adrenal axis to combined dexamethasone/corticotropin-releasing hormone challenge in female borderline personality disorder subjects with a history of sustained childhood abuse," *Biol Psychiatry,* 2002; 52: 1102–12.

[81] H Anisman, L Grimmer, J Irwin et al. (1979), "Escape performance after inescapable shock in selectively bred lines of mice: response maintenance and catecholamine activity," *J Comp Physiol Psychol* 93(2):229-241.

[82] MB Stein, KJ Jang, S Taylor et al. (2002), "Genetic and environmental influences on trauma exposure and posttraumatic stress disorder: a twin study," *Am J Psychiatry* 159(10):1675-1681.

[83] WJ True, J Rice, SA Eisen et al. (1993), "A twin study of genetic and environmental contributions to liability for

posttraumatic stress symptoms," *Arch Gen Psychiatry* 50(4):257-264.

[84] H Xian, SI Chantarujikapong, JF Scherrer et al. (2000), "Genetic and environmental influences on posttraumatic stress disorder, alcohol and drug dependence in twin pairs." *Drug Alcohol Depend* 61(1):95-102.

[85] RH Segman, R Cooper-Kazaz, F Macciardi et al. (2002), "Association between the dopamine transporter gene and posttraumatic stress disorder," *Mol Psychiatry* 7(8):903-907.

[86] RH Segman, N Shefi, T Goltser-Dubner et al. (2005), "Peripheral blood mononuclear cell gene expression profiles identify emergent post-traumatic stress disorder among trauma survivors." *Mol Psychiatry* 10(5):500-513, 425. (In this study by Segman and colleagues, the authors observed peripheral blood mononuclear cell gene expression profiles in individuals seen in the emergency department shortly after a traumatic event and followed one and four months later. They found that gene expression signatures differentiated between individuals who developed PTSD and those who did not.

[87] Charles Portney, M.D. "Intergenerational Transmission of Trauma: An Introduction for the Clinician," *Psychiatric Times*, April 2003, Vol. XX, Issue 4.

[88] RC Kessler, A Sonnega, E Bromet, et al, "Posttraumatic stress disorder in the National Comorbidity Survey," *Arch Gen Psychiatry*. 1995; 52:1048-1060.

[89] Judith Lewis Herman, (1992.) *Trauma and Recovery: The Aftermath of Violence-From Domestic Abuse to Political Terror*. New York: Harper & Row.

[90] Temple Grandin and Margaret M Schariano, *Emergence: Labeled Autistic: A True Story,* Time Warner Book Group-Novato, CA. 2005.

[91] Frank Baum, *Queen Zixi of Ix or The Story of the Magic Cloak,* New York: The Century Company, 1905.

[92] Robert van Reekum, M.D., Chris A Conway, M.D, David Gansler, PhD, Roberta White PhD, David L Bachman, M.D., *Neurobehavioral Study of Borderline Personality Disorder*, J Psychiatry Neuroscience, 1993 May; 18(3): 121-129.

[93] Y Yoshida, T Uchiyama, The clinical necessity for assessing Attention Deficit/Hyperactivity Disorder (AD/HD) symptoms in

children with high-functioning Pervasive Developmental Disorder (PDD). Eur Child Adolesc Psychiatry. 2004 Oct;13(5):307.

[94] Jerold J. Kreisman, & Hal Straus, I Hate You-Don't Leave Me: Understanding the Borderline Personality, New York: Avon Books, 1989.

[95] Ibid.

[96] -Review of research by I. Weinberg, 2000

[97] Judith Lewis Herman, (1992.) Trauma and Recovery: The Aftermath of Violence-From Domestic Abuse to Political Terror. New York: Harper & Row.

[98] Julia A. Golier, M.D., Rachel Yehuda, Ph.D., Linda M. Bierer, M.D., Vivian Mitropoulou, M.A., Antonia S. New, M.D., James Schmeidler, Ph.D., Jeremy M. Silverman, Ph.D. and Larry J. Siever, M.D., "The Relationship of Borderline Personality Disorder to Posttraumatic Stress Disorder and Traumatic Events," Am J Psychiatry 160:2018-2024, November 2003.

[99] Zweig-Frank, "Childhood Sexual Abuse in Relation to Neurobiological Challenge Tests in PTSD with BPD and Normals," *Psychiatric Residency* 06 141 (3).

[100] Zoloft(R) Is the First and Only Treatment Approved for Long-Term Use in Posttraumatic Stress Disorder (PTSD.) FDA Approval Based on Study Showing Significantly Lower Relapse Rates in Men and Women. NEW YORK, Aug. 16 /PRNewswire/ -- Pfizer Inc.

[101] LaNae Valentine, & Leslie L. Feinauer, (1994, January.) "Resilient Abuse Survivors Share Certain Characteristics," *Addiction Letter.* 10 (1) 4.

[102] Robert Brooks, M.D., "How Can Parents Nurture Resilience in Their Children" *Schwablearning.org* (November, 2001.)

[103] A.A. Milne, *The Story of Winnie the Poo,* E.P. Dutton & Co., 1926.

93 C Schmall, "Frontolimbic brain abnormalities in patients with borderline personality disorder: a volumetric magnetic resonance imaging study," *Biol Psychiatry* 2003 Jul 15;54(2):163-71.

[105] M. Driessen, J. Herrmann, et al., "Magnetic resonance imaging volumes of the hypocampus and the amygdala in women with borderline personality disorder and early traumatization," Archives of General Psychiatry 57, no. 12 (2002): 1115-1122.131.

[107] EH Aylward, NJ Minshew, G Goldstein, NA Honeycutt, AM Augustine, KO Yates, et al., "MRI volumes of amygdala and hippocampus in non-mentally retarded autistic adolescents and adults," Neurology 1999; 53: 2145–50.

[108] DC Rojas, JA Smith, TL Benkers, SL Camou, ML Reite, SJ Rogers. "Hippocampus and amygdala volumes in parents of children with autistic disorder," *Am J Psychiatry.* 2004 Nov;161(11):2038-44.

[109] C Schmall, "Frontolimbic brain abnormalities in patients with borderline personality disorder: a volumetric magnetic resonance imaging study," *Biol Psychiatry* 2003 Jul 15;54(2):163-71.

[110] M. Driessen, J. Herrmann, et al., "Magnetic resonance imaging volumes of the hypocampus and the amygdala in women with borderline personality disorder and early traumatization," *Archives of General Psychiatry* 57, no. 12 (2002): 1115-1122.131.

[111] *Arch Gen Psychiatry* 2000 Dec (from Germany). "Magnetic resonance imaging volumes of the hippocampus and the amygdala in women with borderline personality disorder and early traumatization."

[112] *Biol Psychiatry* 2003 Dec 1;54(11):1284-93 (Yale University) "Amygdala hyperreactivity in borderline personality disorder: implications for emotional dysregulation."

[113] Biol Psychiatry 2001 Aug (from Germany) "Evidence of abnormal amygdala functioning in borderline personality disorder: a functional MRI study."

[114] DC Rojas, JA Smith, TL Benkers, SL Camou, ML Reite, SJ Rogers. Hippocampus and amygdala volumes in parents of children with autistic disorder. Am J Psychiatry. (2004) Nov;161(11):2038-44.

[115] EH Aylward, NJ Minshew, G Goldstein, NA Honeycutt, AM Augustine, KO Yates, et al., "MRI volumes of amygdala and hippocampus in non-mentally retarded autistic adolescents and adults," *Neurology* 1999; 53: 2145–50.

[116] Jeffrey Munson; Geraldine Dawson; Robert Abbott; Susan Faja; Sara Jane Webb; Seth D. Friedman; Dennis Shaw; Alan Artru; Stephen R. Dager, *Arch Gen Psychiatry.* 2006;63:686-693.

[117] P.H Soloff., C.C Meltzer, P.J Greer, et al., "A Fenfluramine-activated FD8-PET study of borderline personality disorder," *Biological Psychiatry* 47 (2000): 540.

[118] IK Lyoo, MH Han, DY Cho, "A brain MRI study in subjects with borderline personality disorder," *J Affect Disord* 1998; 50: 235–43.

[119] L Tebartz van Elst, B Hesslinger, T Thiel, et al., "Frontolimbic brain abnormalities in patients with borderline personality disorder: a volumetric magnetic resonance imaging study," *Biol Psychiatry* 2003; 54: 163–71.

[120] *Prog Neuropsychopharmacol Biol Psychiatry* 2004 Mar;28(2):329-41."Neurocognitive function in BPD.

[121] Ludger Tebartz van Elst, Bernd Hesslinger, Thorsten Thiel, Emanuel Geiger, Kerstin Haegele, Louis Lemieux, Klaus Lieb, Martin Bohus, Jürgen Hennig and Dieter Ebert, "Frontolimbic brain abnormalities in patients with borderline personality disorder: a volumetric magnetic resonance imaging study," *Biological Psychiatry,*Volume 54, Issue 2 , 15 July 2003, pages 163-171.

[122] Elizabeth N. Bartmess-LeVasseur and Kathryn Loveland. *Multimedia Textbook in Behavioral Neuroscience.* Rice University.

[123] AE Skodol, LJ Siever, WJ Livesley, JC Gunderson, B Pfohl, TA Widiger, "The Borderline Diagnosis II: biology, genetics and clinical course," *Biological Psychiatry* 2002; 51: 951-63.

[124] A BAILEY; A LECOUTEUR; I GOTTESMAN; P BOLTON; E SIMONOFF; et al., "AUTISM AS A STRONGLY GENETIC DISORDER - EVIDENCE FROM A BRITISH TWIN STUDY," 1995 *PSYCHOLOGICAL MEDICINE* 25 (1): 63-77.

[125] Jeffrey Munson; Geraldine Dawson; Robert Abbott; Susan Faja; Sara Jane Webb; Seth D. Friedman; Dennis Shaw; Alan Artru; Stephen R. Dager
Arch Gen Psychiatry. 2006;63:686-693.

Printed in the United States
101101LV00004B/85/A